SANDINO'S GRAVE
AND OTHER POEMS

Preston M. Browning, Jr.

For my very dear friend Colleen with great admiration and much love —
Preston Browning 6/2/18

WELLSPRING PRESS
ASHFIELD, MASSACHUSETTS

Advanced Praise

"In this wide-ranging book of exquisitely crafted poems, Preston Browning writes, "I long for poets/who speak a mother tongue/meant to connect//…" And that is precisely what he gives us. In classic form, in rhyme and blank verse, from poems that rage against injustice and poems that cherish the most delicate of moments, this poet-activist speaks through our minds to our hearts, connecting all the way. Carry this book with you; when you need that special poem, you will no doubt find it here."

—**Patricia Lee Lewis** leads creative writing workshops and retreats at Patchwork Farm in Westhampton MA and internationally. Her published books of poems include *A Kind of Yellow* and *High Lonesome*, Hedgerow Press.

"Preston Browning is a force of nature and a poet of remarkable range. In this volume of poems and translations, he moves effortlessly from poems of love and courtship to political reckoning. I was consistently transfixed."

—**Steve Almond**, author of *Bad Stories: What the Hell Just Happened to Our Country*

"Browning's poems range from sonnet to elegy to nursery rhyme. Through all the changes, he knows exactly what he is doing: striving to create ' . . . poetry in a language less precious / than that other tongue / that may be just the thing / for communicating with angels.' *Sandino's Grave* welcomes in all of us the angels of listening, and being the better for it."

—**Pat Schneider**, author: *Writing Alone and With Others* and *How the Light Gets In*, both from Oxford University Press, and founder, Amherst Writers & Artists.

"With the humility of years, energized by the eagerness of a youthful, continually questing spirit, Preston Browning's poems speak to a deep affection for the world. His work celebrates his family, honors other writers, and delights in the life of the mind; how its tensions partner with the jokes and ironies of progressing through a human life. Browning is a poet urged by deep concerns with injustice; his work speaks of the need to make right the worst of our humanness, yet his poems continue to hope for a salvageable world. Our unknown future is held dear. Browning's poems, while often erudite, are neither removed nor congested and occasionally have the surprising slants of a trickster.

His translations are a real pleasure; his elegy for Richard Wilbur an homage of true sweetness. Preston Browning is one man yet with many tones of voice; his work is of singular moral heart and mind."

—**Pamela Stewart**, author of The Red Window, Ghost Farm, and Just Visiting

"*Sandino's Grave and Other Poems* by Preston M. Browning, Jr. is eclectic in style and full of wit and wonder. It highlights many of the most important sociopolitical issues of our times, but it does not want for love poems to family and satiric wit. A very vital part of the book is Browning's adept translations of Latin American poets Nicanor Parra, Francisco de Asís Fernández, Otto René Castillo. All in all, it's an edifying and inspiring read, highly recommended."

—**Daniela Gioseffi**, American Book Award winning author, Editor: Eco-Poetry.org

"Preston Browning's *Sandino's Grave and Other Poems* offers the reader the perfectly-ripened poetic fruits of a lifetime of uneasy reflection; as in Wordsworth's paradoxical formula – 'it takes its origin from emotion recollected in tranquility' but nonetheless manifests 'the spontaneous overflow of powerful feelings' – feelings that range from the most irreducibly intimate and private (dealing with the experience of nature, romantic love, family, friendships) to others that emerge from a public or civil idiom that most contemporary poets seem to have forgotten how to speak (dealing with America politics and its disastrous effects on Vietnam and the countries of Latin America). The diversity of genres and tones on display – tender love poems and elegies to the Virginia spring-times of the poet's youth, subtle analyses of conflicted friendships, impassioned political confessions brimming with anger and black comedy – testify equally to Browning's wide-ranging poetic influences and to a fully-engaged life – which the book brings to a truly eloquent synthesis with lucid and appropriately fiery translations from some of the Latin American authors that inspired Browning's own poems. In reading *Sandino's Grave* one can't not think of Pablo Neruda."

—**James Prakash Younger**, Associate Professor, Department of English, Coordinator of Literature and Film Track, Film Studies Program, and InterArts Program, Trinity College, Hartford, CT

"Nestled among these poems (some personal, some political, some pictorial, some picturesque, including eight translations of Central and South American poems) is a paean to the poet's deceased wife, 'Someone to Call You 'Darling,' tiny in length, but revealing the extraordinary in the ordinary, releasing ripples resonating continually with time. The poet has been for 77 years recognizing this luminescence, but time (in a different context) serves his twenty-year-old daughter with 'a shoreless ocean to be drunk.' There is also a diptych of sonnets, 'Oedipus' and 'Jocasta,' each a pearl standing alone, but so much more in their tragic dance together. Add to those a tip of the hat to T. S. Eliot, a lament for a dying planet, an ironic riposte to the 'Land of the Free,' and a personal favorite 'Me and My Woman' (to mention a few), and you have a collection that dazzles with a difference with every dip."

—**Boman Desai**, author of *The Memory of Elephants* and *TRIO: a Novel Biography of the Schumanns and Brahms*

"In his collection *Sandino's Grave and Other Poems*, Preston Browning asks, Who knows the source of wisdom? His poems provide multiple pathways to an answer. Whether he is probing politics and history, or elegizing a loved one, or immersing himself in the changing seasons, he shows us what it means to think and to feel with a whole heart."

—**Jennifer C. Barber**, author of *Works on Paper*; editor, Salamander

"*Sandino's Grave* is an all-encompassing triumph of erudition, craft, and political convictions from octogenarian poet Preston Browning. His subjects range from domestic love and violence to climate change to heroic resistance to autocratic rule and gringo imperialism in Central America. Closer to home he offers views on the Jim-Crow South of his youth and Black Lives Matter. No free verse poet should be put off by Browning's insistence on rhyme and meter; there is linguistic dexterity to be found in this collection and mastery of tradition forms—from sonnet to ode to limerick to Wordsworthian elegy to haiku. In one epistolary poem he convincingly defends his passionate embrace of political activism against highbrow Freudian analysis; then, in another, effortlessly changes modality to pen a takedown ditty equal to any by Calvin Trillin:

'Humpty Trumpty sat on a fence
his ample backsides covered by Pence.
But the Russians grabbed him
and shaved off his hair,
lo and behold
there was "no there there.'

Browning concludes this generous collection with a sampling of his admired Latin American poets in sensitive and scrupulous translations."

—**Mark Pawlak**, author most recently of *Reconnaissance*, also poet and co-editor of Hanging Loose Press

"In this stirring and evocative collection, poet and activist, Preston Browning sets his unflinching gaze on a broad swath of subjects with relationships at their core: international and intra-national relations, intimate relationships, and humankind's relationship to the Divine and to the natural world….Browning never surrenders to resignation and in this collection there is ample reason to rejoice and be hopeful, for … love, love hides herself/waiting to be surprised/ by him who knows her name (from 'Elegy for an Eighty-Year-Old Southern Romantic')."

—**Arlyn Miller**, Editor in Chief, Poetic License Press

Copyright © 2018 by Prestion M. Browning, Jr.
Published in the United States by:
Wellspring Press
P. O. Box 2006, Ashfield, MA   01330

Cover design: The Turning Mill, Palenville, New York   12463

Cover image: Solentiname, Nicaragua by Rosa Pineda
Sandino's Grave and Other Poems

ISBN: 978-0-692-13006-3
1. American Poetry   2. Latin American Poetry Translations

SANDINO'S GRAVE AND OTHER POEMS
CONTENTS

HOW I CAME TO POETRY xv

I.

A Wise Man Named John 1

Love Poem 3

Not Exactly Love 4

Oedipus 5

Jocasta 6

A Poet Surpassing Great 7

April in Chicago 8

Erotic April 10

Generational Voices 11

Short Hill Mountain 13

Tongues of Men . . . and of Women 15

For My Third Daughter on Her Twentieth Birthday 17

Spring Song 18

Me and My Woman 19

The Love Song of Any Aging Male 20

To a Dying Planet 24

Christmas Eve Near Black Holes 25

II.

Mr. Jefferson on Sixty-Third Street 29
Sandino's Grave 31
Love It and Leave It 33
Letter to an Old, Esteemed, and Somewhat Estranged Friend 34
Pledge of Allegiance 38
Vietnam Christmas Recollected 40
New World Order 42
Epitaph for Ronald Reagan 48
El Colonialismo a la Mode 51
Land of the Free 53

III.

Translations
Otto René Castillo

Intelectuales Apolíticos/Apolitical Intellectuals 59/62
Viudo de Mundo/Widower of the World 65/66

Francisco de Asís Fernández

Palabras de Mujeres/Women's Words 67/69
Memoria del Sueño/Memory of the Dream 71/73

Nicanor Parra

El Túnel/The Tunnel 75/78
La Víbora/The Viper 81/85
Recuerdos de Juventud/Memories of Youth 89/91

IV.

The Eyes of the Children of Solentiname 95
Sound and Fury 97
The Baptism 98
3 AM 100
Grandmother 101
Millennium Weather 106
Managua '88 108
Bottled Brotherhood: My Uncle Sam 109
Had I the Poet's Ear 110
I Love To Spin a Rhyme 111
Elegy for an Eighty-Year-Old Southern Romantic ... 112
Someone to Call You Darling 114

WITH GRATITUDE 115

ABOUT THE AUTHOR 131

ORDERING & CONTACT INFORMATION 133

*This book is dedicated to all
the women in my life:
my grandmother, Cornelia Cabell Stephenson
my mother, Gertrude Stephenson Browning
my favorite aunt, Annie Cabell Stephenson
my aunt, Virginia Browning Wood
my sister, Anne Browning Ripley
my wife, Ann Virginia Hutt Browning
my daughters:
Katharine Hutt Browning
Sarah Goldsmith Browning
Rachel Cabell Browning
my granddaughter, Grace Browning
my nieces:
Martha Browning Cordell
Constance Ripley
Elizabeth Ripley Stromeyer
and Jenny Brown,
housekeeper and faithful supporter*

Cornelia Cabell Stephenson

Gertrude Stephenson Browning

Ann Virginia Hutt Browning

Katharine Hutt Browning

Sarah Goldsmith Browning

Grace Browning

Rachel Cabell Browning

'Tis few indeed who see thee as thou art
Too beautiful and warm for light of day,
Substance pure suffused in every part
With morning-glory tints, unearthly spray.
Delight divine to one who glances casts
About thy path, or from thy lips perceives
In muted tones, like echoes from the past,
A voice, which fading, blesses ere it leaves.
And if thy beauty be above men's sight
Thy perfect soul not meant for careless eyes,
Can I in unmoved calm survey its light
Content with present joys the grave belies?
If this be all then were it Hell to be
Allowed such bliss short of eternity.

(Composed in Columbia, Missouri, October, 1958, after my first date with Ann Virginia Hutt, who two weeks later became my fiancée and the following June my bride)

How I Came to Poetry (or poetry came to me)

Many of the poems in this book were written during the Vietnam War era or soon afterwards. To say that I was distracted by the crimes committed in my name in that far-off country would not quite do justice to the effects that horrendous slaughter of civilians had upon my spirit. Two of my poems, "Love It and Leave It" and "Vietnam Christmas Recollected" both reflect the anguish I endured as I watched hundreds of thousands of civilians killed and much of the Vietnam countryside virtually destroyed by endless bombardments and use of Agent Orange. What I saw on television or learned from my reading led to the conclusion that once again the country I loved was fighting on the wrong side.

My longstanding concern about my country's history of invasions, interventions, and occupations plus support for dictators beginning in the early 20th century, principally in Latin America and the Caribbean, but not exclusively there, was greatly intensified when I became aware of an ongoing struggle in Nicaragua to overthrow a brutal and rapacious dictator, Anastacio Somoza. Somoza's National Guard, virtually his private army, was primed to capture, torture, and murder any who opposed their boss. Like many another "strong man" of Latin America, this one's greed knew no bounds.

By the 1980s, his wealth was estimated at about a billion dollars, this in a country where millions lived with no education, no health care, and no political representation. His support by the U.S. government was taken for granted as was its support for other repressive, often bloody regimes south of the border.

This may be an appropriate moment at which to provide additional historical data in order to make clearer such matters as the reasons for the presence of a U. S. Marine officer in Nicaragua in 1927 ("New World Order"). There are, in fact, a number of Nicaraguan references or images in this volume, e.g., the cover image and the poem "The Eyes of the Children of Solentiname." This historical data will also make clear an answer, for those asking, "Who in the hell was Sandino?" It should also clarify the reasons for the bitterness of the tone of such poems as "New World Order" and "Epitaph for Ronald Reagan."

Marine Corp General Smedley Butler can serve as our major source at this juncture. The Marines occupied Nicaragua from 1913 to 1933, and, when he retired in the mid-thirties, Butler wrote several articles describing precisely what was involved in his activities in that country as well as in other Central American lands. His testimony will no doubt come as a shocker to most Americans as he describes himself as a gringo "enforcer": "During this period I spent most of my time being a high-class muscle man for Big Business, for Wall Street and the bankers. In short I was a racketeer for capitalism." Butler comments that he outdid Al Capone in grand style; Capone could ravage only three counties, while he, General Butler, lead the way in the "rape" of five Central American republics.

Now Sandino enters the picture, for with a band of barefooted peasants armed with antique rifles and machetes, he and his followers fought Smedley Butler's men to a draw. When the Marines withdrew from Nicaragua they left behind the National Guard, headed by Anastacio Somoza. Tricked into believing that Somoza wished for a peace accord, Sandino met with this petty mobster and was assassinated, thereafter becoming a national hero.

When in the late seventies a group of Nicaraguans, many of them highly educated individuals joined by students and ordinary citizens of both sexes, organized to violently overthrow the Somoza regime, they quite naturally chose to call themselves Sandinistas.

The Sandinistas triumphed in that struggle, but tens of thousands of their enemies escaped to Honduras, other Central American countries, Mexico, or Miami and became known as "contras," contra being the Spanish word for against. Determined to overthrow the Sandinista government, the contras, now supplied, armed, and paid by the C.I.A., waged a ruthless war against the Sandinistas. Although Ronald Reagan described them as "the moral equivalent of the

Founding Fathers," the contras were thugs and employed the methods of thugs to achieve their goals—torture, rape, assassination, destruction of schools and health clinics, any signs that the new socialist government was creating a more healthy, more humane Nicaragua.

I visited Nicaragua in 1984 and 1988. On the first of these trips, I was delighted with what I found. Despite the costs of the war, with young soldiers killed and contra attacks on two fronts, in Managua where I spent most of my time, there was a noticeable mood of hope, with plans underway for achieving a genuinely new society where the poorest citizen received the same respect and attention as the richest. One morning I visited a hospital where a gringo doctor led me on a tour and I learned, for example, that no woman about to give birth was ever turned away even if three women had to share a bed.

Later on the street, I was accosted by a man whose clothes suggested that he was probably a campesino. He greeted me and pointed to a pen protruding from my shirt pocket. I could replace the pen for less than 50 cents, so I gave him the pen. Then he pointed to the pad I was carrying. "Why not?" I said to myself. "Contribute to the literacy campaign." So I handed him the pad. And he signed his name! That was all. Then he returned both of the items I thought I was giving him. This exchange came to symbolize for me the deeper, I think it fair to say, spiritual, meaning of this revolution. What the Sandinistas had conferred upon this man was a sense of self-worth. Of dignity. And right then I fell in love with Nicaragua. And with the revolutionary government.

When I returned four years later, the mood was utterly different; an air of depression was noticeable everywhere. The contra war continued, inflation had gone through the roof, there was scarcity of many necessities, from cooking oil to toilet paper (the U.S. blockade saw to that), and I was told to carry little money at night since robberies were common. On the first visit, I had walked the streets of Managua at all hours, feeling completely safe.

I returned home filled with anger and ashamed that America's leaders were capable of such deception and cruelty, with slick con men such as Col. Oliver North scheming to convince members of Congress and the public that the Sandinistas were the source of Nicaragua's ills and that our tax dollars were well-spent supporting the contras. Thus, when I wrote about these matters, my tone normally reflected a bitterness rooted in a sense of betrayal. I was like a deceived and betrayed lover. The betrayers, I eventually understood, were, as T. S. Eliot would have put it, "not men enough to be damned."

So far as I can remember now, I wrote little poetry at the time but when I later composed "Epitaph for Ronald Reagan" and "New World Order," this period of corruption and lies was very much on my mind. In fact, I've continued to reflect on Nicaragua and friends there—the painters and artisans of Solentiname—during a time of unrest in Central America. In the news reports of Central American refugees fleeing to the north, I've heard no mention of the fact that those escaping brutality and violence are from countries with rightwing, repressive governments such as El Salvador and Honduras, where the Obama administration accepted the overthrowing of a democratic government, not from the socialist Nicaragua. A poem or two about these young persons will be forthcoming, but far too late to find a berth in *Sandino's Grave and Other Poems*.

Many who have read the contents of this book comment on its variety—fairly long poems, very short ones; love poems, harsh, bitter poems; poems with rhyme and fairly regular meter, poems that are obviously free verse; poems that might evoke a slightly sinister laugh, e.g., "Pledge of Allegiance," with its reference to "Humpty Trumpty" and his "ample backsides" sitting on a fence and poems that are all sweetness and light.

Though I have written a good bit of prose about nature and the dangers humanity faces from global warming, my readers will find little here that could be called "nature poetry." Also, there is the matter of time, since I am now in my late eighties. There is much that distinguishes the 1958 sonnet for Ann, which opens this book, from the poems written quite recently, such as "Bottled Brotherhood." A world of thought, experience, learning, teaching, family life, loving, and grief separates the respective eras from which these two poems came.

Now a word about the translations:

In the mid-eighties, when I was still teaching at the University of Illinois at Chicago, a colleague in Latin American Studies, who was preparing a book of translations, asked if I'd like to try my hand. This was something I had never previously done, but as a lover of language who had studied Spanish at prep school and each semester at Washington & Lee, I found the idea attractive. At first I thought it might be something of a chore, but I had a free summer to devote to the project. Not far into the first morning, I discovered that, rather than being a chore, the flipping through my English-Spanish dictionary and choosing the right word for a metaphor for capitulation or a synonym for ecstasy was nothing but joy. Thus by September I had about forty translations. I was attracted especially to the Guatemalan poet Otto René Castillo and the Nicaraguan writer Francisco de Asís Fernández, both of whom had fought with their respective country's revolutionary forces. Castillo's poem "Apolitical Intellectuals" is one of the best-known and most-loved poems from a Central American writer of the twentieth century. After being captured and tortured for four days by the Guatemalan army, Castillo, at age 31, was burned at the stake. I translated perhaps 15 of his poems, most of which bore some relationship to his country's struggle to overthrow a brutal military dictatorship led by a general who was later convicted of genocide.

* * *

Francisco de Asís Fernández volunteered, as did thousands of others, to take part in the armed combat to oust the Somoza dictatorship. His poetry is rooted in that experience, reflecting a passionate love of country and contempt for those who sell out for wealth or power. His poem, "Women's Words," reveals the degree to which that struggle was a communal fight for liberty and democracy. He was the author of several books of poems, among them *The Passion of Memory* and *Tree of Life*.

* * *

Until I retired from teaching in 1998 and moved to Massachusetts the following year, the Chilean writer Nicanor Parra was a total mystery to me. It's true that I had been given a book of his entitled *Poems and Antipoems* some years earlier by Dia Cirillo, the daughter of Nancy Cirillo, a colleague and dear friend. Dia knew of my interest in Latin American poetry and brought me the Parra volume after an academic year in Chile. I probably scanned it but did not at the time find Parra's style especially interesting, though the notes on the cover described him as famous in South America. Fortunately, I brought the book with me when Ann and I made our first visit to Guatemala in the winter of 1999.

When, some months earlier, I was preparing for retirement, I received a phone call from one of my favorite teachers at the University of Chicago, James E. Miller, Jr. of the English Department. Jim had heard of my upcoming retirement and wanted to present to Ann and me a gift to help celebrate that occasion—a one-month stay at a house that he and his wife Barbara owned in Antigua, Guatemala. It didn't take us long to say Yes. Soon after arriving in that lovely small city, both Ann and I registered at a language "school," I to recover some of the ability I once had for the spoken language, Ann, who had had many years of French, but no Spanish, to gain a modest speaking facility. One morning when I was laboring mightily to memorize irregular verbs, I felt totally bored and said to my instructor, "José, I'm going out of my mind with boredom. Would you help me with translations?" José said Yes and the next day I showed up with Parra's little book. From that point on we spent an hour each morning with Señor Parra, and I came back to Massachusetts with the three translations included here.

Nicanor Parra is a strange bird. And one whose poetry I should not like. A scientist who studied at Brown and Oxford, Parra began to write poetry in the forties and, having been influenced by Whitman whom he read while at Brown, as well as Kafka, Parra created a new kind of literature. This was a literature that rejected unambiguously the romanticism of nineteenth century Spanish and Latin American poetry, that came increasingly to take as subject matter very ordinary everyday things or symbols like the cross which he treated irreverently. The book from which the three translations included here are taken is entitled *Poems and Antipoems* and might be considered a sort of declaration of war against all that makes traditional poetry beautiful. Here in five short lines, Parra states his case against tradition: "For half a century/Poetry was the paradise/Of the solemn fool/Until I came along/And built my roller coaster."

As I indicate in my poem, "Had I the Poet's Ear," I love the work of Donne and Milton and Keats and Yeats and Robert Frost and Langston Hughes and Gwendolyn Brooks and derive great pleasure from searching for rhyming words to create a sonnet. Yet I have to acknowledge that I also enjoyed greatly translating Parra's antipoems and admire the courage of this rebel who took on the practice of hundreds of years. And won. Parra's reputation grew over the decades and by the time of his death in early 2018, he was recognized as one of the foremost literary artists of his era.

* * *

I am sometimes asked why I write poetry? I answer that I write poetry because on bleak January mornings it cheers me to play with words. I write poetry because, while composing under a blossoming apple tree in May, it reminds me of my wife, Ann, who designed the charming renovation of an old carriage house where we lived for many years and where I now reside with unspeakable pleasure. I write poetry because to do so provides an opportunity to think about the past. Not that I *live* in the past. That would be a foolish waste of time. To think about the human family's past serves to deepen one's appreciation of the race's extraordinary creative gifts, among other things, in music, the visual arts, and literature.

There is the personal past, too, and whether joyous or sad, recollections of past happenings in the poet's life may, with luck, lead to a kind of E.E. Cummings moment of affirmation and thanksgiving—not necessarily to a personal divinity as in his case:

> I thank You God for most this amazing
> day: for the leaping greenly spirit of trees
> and a blue true dream of sky, and for everything
> which is natural which is infinite which is yes

Just to be alive and thinking is a grand miracle. Writing poetry is a sort of yes to the yes of creation, and thus my final answer to why I write poetry is simply this: it's what a person does if he is in love with the Earth, in love with human life, and in love with language. It's a love affair so glorious as to be beyond description.

I.

A Wise Man Named John

for John Yungblut—in memoriam

Who knows the source
of wisdom?
Aeschylus and Sophocles
said suffering.
You had your share of that,
I am certain.

Yet you must have been born
under Gemini,
for in you wisdom
had its twin—goodness.
Were they spawned
at the same moment,
identical, sisters
to your gentleness?

You possessed a rare talent:
to speak with authority
and yet gently.
To speak to the heart
and yet gently.
To speak truth
in a world addicted
to velvet lies,
yet gently.

Gentleman.
Gentle man.
Our language,
like our hearts,
is confused.
(Recently I heard a
killer of eight women
referred to as
"This gentleman.")

Can one be wise
though not gentle. . .
or good?
You left too soon, John,
and I forgot to ask the question.

Love Poem

What is encompassed
in the view of my mind
is you. The pulsating
hard, hungry feel of you,
the gentle, hesitant,
awkward touch of your hands.
Can I, should I, will I,
at this particular
moment and in this place
come near to you? Signal!
There is no repeating
a love moment in time.

Not Exactly Love

I want to write a poem about love.
Not movie-time love,
nor squishy, Wonder-Bread love.
No, not love!
That battered word.
Compassion-love.
Com-passion.
Yes, with passion.
But passion with & for & unto.
Passion with hurt.
Passion that stretches out & out & out,
to something like a world,
like a galaxy,
like a universe.
Riding a rainbow.
No!
Riding a whirlwind.

Oedipus

Your neck was fitted for the hangman's noose
a thousand years before Jocasta's sport
with stout Laius bred a dire report
that you, cursed child, would cook the family's goose.

Bold struggles, bold luck did your mind seduce,
till very Fate your fancy seemed to court;
how nimbly ample rope became too short,
as luck and mother wit conspired for foul abuse.

Oh, Oedipus, proud Oedipus, what use
to flee the womb that was your last resort?
That land, wise Sigmund said, where lay the port
your vessel homed for till its sails hung loose.

Are you, then, "Swollen Foot," with ribs intact,
not Adam, dread father of what men lack?

Jocasta

Oh, awful fate, oh, pity, grief and shame,
to bear the bearer of the gods' foul curse;
to cast him out with neither teats to nurse
nor graven tombstone fit to praise his name.

That wily stranger who the Sphinx did tame,
you bedded him for better or for worse;
your wedding joy was sung in Attic verse
till child and husband answered you the same.

Ah, reckless, sad Jocasta, who's to blame
for loving him who loved you in reverse;
your piteous fable ages still rehearse:
lament and woe and fear, alas, and fame.

And in the palace where you tied the knot,
did you find the answer that you had forgot?

A Poet Surpassing Great

for Richard Wilbur—in memoriam

I know a man named Richard,
who plays with feet and rhyme
each time he hits a metaphor,
you'll hear the church bells chime.

He's a neighbor is this Richard,
whose verse is passing fine,
it's graced by singing meter
and wit that's quite sublime.

You'd think it came from Heaven,
or some other lofty realm;
but truth be told,
it's from the soul
of him! of him! of him!

April in Chicago

In Chicago
spring is never sure of itself,
no bravado,
no cocksure certainty
that daffodils
will compete for attention
when tomorrow's sun
peeks through skylights
and lands,
dazed and stammering,
somewhere between lake
and school yard.

Farther south,
in Virginia, for instance,
spring's arrival
announces itself
like Beethoven's Ninth,
the whole mad orchestra
roused to frenzy:
strings, horns,
and percussion rising
toward heavenly consummation,
sensuousness
in perpetual uproar,
wedding things heard,
seen, and smelled to things
only longed for.

Spring in those parts
overwhelms with excess—
redbud, magnolia, rhododendron,
cherry and narcissus
wooing eye, mind,
and olfactory organs
to such a pitch
of concentrated delight
that lapses in attention
seem blasphemous.

In Chicago,
spring is winter's
timid step-daughter,
almost apologetic
for occupying the same
space, for asking
to renew the lease.

Erotic April

(Recollections)

What you feel in the morning
is not so different from
a whirlwind
in the hinterland of the mind.

Purple blossoms file
through branches
of frosted apple trees
suffused with perfume,
odors as pungent
as long-stored cabbages,
while strumpet tulips
call beneath kite strings,
lips crying, "Kiss me, Oh!"

Springtime down south
consumes you,
leaving only a memory,
a report from a world
voluptuous and sad.

Generational Voices

This early June morning
four honkers flew over our house
as the cold rain fell
on the hill beyond,
and Ruth Stone,
a poet whose strong
southern voice
carried generations of affection
and sturdy grace,
spoke of her mother
reading Tennyson's "In Memoriam"
to her when she was
not yet three.

Ruth and her granddaughter, Bianca,
at sixteen, herself a poet,
have been reading to schoolchildren
in the hill towns of western Massachusetts
where many voices compete
via radio, TV, and telephone,
honkers intent upon
firing minds and stirring emotions
in a dot.com world
this eighty-five year old
neither celebrates nor admires,
an inevitable disconnect
which one need not be past eighty

or to have heard Tennyson's
melancholy voice
when hardly out of diapers
in order to understand.

Among schoolchildren,
this team recites,
employing ordinary words
to connect ordinary things:
the rain, the geese, the hill,
the loss of loved ones,
the pain and joy of being sixteen,
the daily gifts of an eighty-fifth year.

Short Hill Mountain

for Preston III

Up there you sit, alone, remote, above
sharp wineberry thorns and tangled, creeping vines;
deer trails cross over midway up your side
and near the ridge bobcats (some say) make love,
when black midnight wind soughs
through beech and pines;
while farther down, the grapevines hang astride
a plunging stream which like a swallow's flight
descends to earth as bound for nether parts,
then checks its haste and curls to ebbing tide
just where the bobwhite quail zoom out of sight
among the dogwood, oak, and redbud hearts,
and motes of light that fern fronds almost hide.

When April clouds let down their hair and weep
upon your epaulets of leaf and moss,
your swelling majesty appears to keep
no recollection of dark winter's loss.

Then violets are born beneath the vines
and rhododendrons scent the air above,
as urgent sap and feverish bee combine
to frame a question apropos of love.

Whence comes this wish to lavish springtime's joy
on buds and blossoms all ephemeral;
have you no fear such wastage will alloy
the strength you need to face the sovereign fall?

Yet summer's green retains its green so long
that August light reflects May's vaunting hues;
and grapevines shape a sheet of blowing notes
that trick from nature nature's primal song.

But when October's yellow shades to blues,
or browns or blacks depending on the light;
you sit there still, enrobed in gloomy pride,
unmoved, apparently—impervious as night.

Who knows if you're as lonely as I thought?
For round your head grave eagles sometimes glide.
Who knows but what you share the quails' delight
and to the bobcat's heart your lusts confide?

Some say your soul is hard as hardest flint.
I say you're old with nothing to repent.

Tongues of Men ... and of Women

I used to read them,
the poems in *American Poetry Review*
and other high-tone journals,
and some of them I understood
and admired,
but most seemed designed to baffle,
the guiding principle being,
I suppose,
the fewer readers who know
what's going on
the better the poem.

But I live in a world
where people die of hunger,
40,000 children each day,
and women are raped—
how many each minute?—
and mothers weep for sons
lost to greed and old men's
dreams of grandeur.

Maybe they speak
that other language
on the dry hillsides of Mars
but in the world I know
too many die
because they cannot be heard—
in any language.

So I long for poets
who speak a mother tongue
meant to connect:
Pablo Neruda, Ernesto Cardenal, Susan Sanchez,
Langston Hughes, and Adrienne Rich,
poets not ashamed
to speak their minds
to those who know
that what the world wants
is poetry in a language less precious
than that other tongue
that may be just the thing
for communicating with angels.

For My Third Daughter on Her Twentieth Birthday

for Rachel

How slow they seem, those creeping twenty years,
and time's a beggar with ever-empty cup;
you'd think a hundred million light years
were but a prelude to the filling up.

Just wait until you're forty, my fair lady,
that cup will then begin to overflow,
with seconds, hours and days so plaguy hurried
you'd not believe they know the sense of slow.

And when you reach that benchmark age of sixty,
cool time's a vulture squatting on the sill,
with patience rarified by ceaseless watching,
the poise of one who always gets his fill.

Yet twenty's not an age for dark commotion,
nor thoughts of gray or chilly, flinching funk;
pretend that twenty twenties are your portion,
and time a shoreless ocean to be drunk.

Spring Song

When crocuses and lilacs woo coquettish spring
and new-fallen green arrests each vagrant eye;
when blackbirds play at arrant knaves and kings
and kite strings croon a wanton lullaby;
then charmed chords alarm my arid soul,
whose winter sleep no sprightly visions knew,
and once again the heart-bells start their toll
of April joy, May laughter, and you.

Me and My Woman

When me and my woman are singing the blues,
even January sunshine comes as bad news.
When me and my woman are going for blood,
diamonds and rubies have the luster of mud.

When me and my woman are coughing up hate,
the words on our tongues burn like coals on a grate.
When me and my woman begin twisting the knife,
there's anger enough to get you twenty-to-life.

But when me and my woman are loving again,
February's icicles are warm to the skin.
When me and my woman have laid down in peace,
fearsome tigers turn to puddles of grease.

The Love Song of Any Aging Male

(Apologies to Mr. Eliot)

Let us go now,
you and me,
in search of mermaids,
in the sea.

To catch a troll,
behind the stars,
or release fireflies,
trapped in jars.

Let's go quickly,
along that street,
where boys seek girls
and lovers meet.

In cities like
old New Orleans,
where dowdy ladies
dress like queens.

And krewes parade
throughout the Quarter,
tantalizing
each son and daughter.

Oh, do not tell me
you're afraid,
of No! No! No!
from an elder maid.

Come with me,
before the dawn,
to drink some ale
and eat a prawn.

To seek relief
from mad desire,
hear soothing music
played on a lyre.

    In that noisy upscale bar,
the chicks all giggle, "How bald you are!"

And if the lady
you so wish,
decides to be
your special dish.

And turns a blind eye
to your hair,
long gone now,
beyond repair.

And says, "I think
I'll try again,
though you're no prize,
I'll risk the pain.

"Of love that's never,
never sure;
and by the way,
do you snore?

"And can you wait
for love's reprise,
when I cough
and while I sneeze?

"And when a grandchild
climbs your knees,
you'll reply to her
Please! Please! Please!

"With kisses warm
and bon-bons sweet,
although she treads
upon your feet?"

So tell me now
a story true,
how older men
should always woo.

A gentle lady,
not too old,
in manner sure
but not too bold.

But bold enough
to win the day,
and frighten rivals
far away.

One can't be sure,
but I will wager,
the following plan
might finally cage her.

Be bold, yes,
but a little coy,
don't profess your love,
like a lovesick boy.

And let her dally,
let her toy;
protracted longing
will spice your joy.

Let patience be
your faithful guide,
to win a lover,
if not a bride.

To a Dying Planet

You were generous,
unstinting, mad to nurture,
forgiving,
hospitable as a Greek.
You took abuse.
You sickened.
On your knees you coughed,
strangling on soot and dark slime.

Some took notice.
Most took as always,
took with both hands—
like Flaubert's heroine
stuffing the precious powder
toward her heart
till breath was stilled.

You struggled to outlive them.
Anyone seeing you from afar
might have believed
your watery blue veins
a sign of stoic undauntedness.

At your burial
galaxies sang of your fortitude.
No word was spoken
of the killers' end.

Christmas Eve near Black Holes

This Christmas Eve
trickles down
between Greek verbs
bound in a cosmic
vacuum cleaner.

"NOVA" mingles
with *logos*,
galaxies become
bread of heaven.
Mangers twist
nonsense rhymes
toward blinding light.

In one corner
of the universe
the news outshines
the darkness
till sheep
have no map
of gathering day.

What remains,
remains forever
stoppered
in a tiny bottle.

Message and medium,
coaxed by ether,
drawn toward black holes,
resisted to the last.

II.

Mr. Jefferson on 63rd Street
(Chicago's South Side)

for Fred Stern (l929-l992)—in memoriam

"Devil!" he shouted in my ear
approaching me from behind,
thus breaking my reverie of President Jefferson
seated at his desk composing a letter
to President Adams concerning
the "natural aristocracy,"
an association in which both
held charter membership.
Not wealth or birth, he maintained,
but wisdom and integrity
mark those deserving the trust
and respect of their fellow citizens.

Casting a look of contempt
over his shoulder
this immaculately dressed brother
sailed past me toward the El
and then, as if remembering
the shuffling bundle of rags we'd both
skirted a moment before,
he reversed his field and,
like the Duke crossing some dusty street
of a cardboard Warner Brothers town,
he bore down on me,

eyes merry with venom,
until the split second
when the draw came naturally,
the thumb and forefinger delivering
the preordained message
of vengeance and justice:
"Pow!" "Pow!" "Pow!"

This angry black man,
whose very pores breathed outrage—
where was he in Mr. Jefferson's blessed fellowship?

A few minutes later,
now riding the El
toward a rendezvous with twenty faces, all white,
where we would discuss Mr. Jefferson's letter
and debate the chances of
an aristocracy of virtue
surviving competition with
"Now h e e e e e e e e r z Johnny,"
the angry young brother
refused to stop shooting.

Sandino's Grave

The maple leaves,
fired in October's
treacherous oven,
spin and tell me nothing.

From here to you,
resting uneasily
beneath Managua's rubble,
is more than miles.

You receive their blood,
those who ask for bread
and wait for stones.
October's wind cannot reach you
and their cries are carried over the lake,
like crows careening toward Granada.

Patriot or bandit, you eluded them,
the Yankees, astonished by such contempt
for their demand that you bend the knee.
Crazy Horse, Geronimo, Sitting Bull
peer through early morning mists,
dumb at your apotheosis.

Dollar signs circle your neck,
hangman's nooses for all your sons,
as the Great White Father
spills coffee in a beggar's cup.

Tired bones refuse to wear jewelry,
hours wait for no minutes etched
on cathedral sundials
five centuries ago.

Minutes care nothing
for the occupier's whip,
hours spit phlegm and stutter,
years stagger in broken pride.

What's left?
Shadows and the wind,
shadows and the leaves,
shadows and the sun.

Your sun rises early.

Love It and Leave It

Somewhere between the Gulf of Tonkin and My Lai
you began to leave it. You want, it's true,
to love it. Impossible! Each day new
treachery blights the flower. Will you cry?
Brave men don't cry. Your hand fumbles a door.
Sad retreat, as your heart shouts, "They lie!" "They lie!

They also entertain. Thus with a sigh
you try to accept: Her beauty's that of a whore.
How hard to let go, refuse, say goodbye.
Where love once lived, the new lodger's name is "Hate"?
Where love once lived, rough grief is now the mate
that taunts the writhing love that will not die.

Deceit! Deceit! Most choose to believe it.
You can't. You try, and cry, and cannot leave it.

Letter to an Old, Esteemed, and Somewhat Estranged Friend

for P. H.

Your advice—to avoid the political—
was kindly meant and sound.
How I wish that I could have taken it.
Could have found a nook,
an academic cocoon tranquil enough
to still my raging complaint
against Lear's daughters,
a harbor bewitching enough to whelm
my readiness to enter roiling waters.

"Why do you pursue these fierce chimeras,
squandering your talent
on fevered dreams of nowhere?"
you might have asked but didn't.

Had I replied "I don't know,"
you would have guessed I lied.
And had I said,
"Some sort of belief drives me there,"
the slow nodding of your head,
leaving worlds unsaid, might still be as much
as we could hope to know.

But suppose we had another day
and another very different way
to examine and expose all the reasons
why tenaciously I chose a briary path to travel by.

Let's pretend that you,
a friend's kind of friend,
and I, a not entirely ordinary kind of guy,
undertook to find the secret springs
that feed white lava to my boiling mind.
Where would we begin?
"With my anger," I might say,
which you've seldom seen,
though it's a region where others you know
have often been.

"Yes, I thought you intended
analytical inquiry,"
you might interpose.
And I wouldn't be offended
if you were to suppose that thoughtful probing
of the opening of my childhood reliquary
could yield faint illuminations
of that awe-full battlefield.

And if we could, together, explore
the sources of my belief—
my southern upbringing,
the mute, vacant children
with their 1930s eyes and bellies,
my farmer father saving his land by selling Chevrolets
late into the mosquito-bitten Saturday nights,
the weekly hearing of Isaiah, Amos and Jeremiah,
the habitual excoriation of the callous rich,
my gentle mother on her weekly rounds
to invalids and shantytowns
what would we discover?

That my anger
is displaced resentment
against an authoritarian father,
drunk with anxiety about the Bank?
Would Freud, peering vulture-like
into my overwrought psyche,
assisted by a corps of expensively-trained clinicians—
would the good Doktor
give the final quietus to my pain,
by convincing me, once and for all,
that it's only an obsession?

Would the voices relent, would the commands
of prophets fade into whirlwinds?
Would the distended bellies
convert to fetching *Playgirl* profiles?
Would the stumps of my Nicaraguan friends,
Manuel and Juana, grow wings?

Would the eyes no longer haunt, the screams
no longer awaken me in the night,
the breasts of women sliced by "freedom fighters"
no longer glide by at daybreak,
the genitals of campesinos whose crime was saying,
"I love the Revolution because it gave me land,"
no longer choke my evening meal,
the sobs of young women for their lover-husbands
disemboweled for tending the coffee groves
no longer contaminate my own love-making?
Would these yield to an analytic legerdemain,
an apocalyptic waving of a wand,
the ultimate, end-all, millennium-proof dose
of treatment?
And would I be well?

Pledge of Allegiance

"I hate this country
    just hate it."
Phyllis, almost ninety,
    gentlewoman, Quaker.
"Shootings every other month,
    endless wars."
"I hate America, fuck America."
    Maria, poet, hardly thirty.
"I hate living in such a violent place."

Endless violence.
Endless ignorance.
Elections endless, too.

Endless spectacle,
inexhaustible, in all sizes and colors,
    exactly what the doctor ordered
        for atrophied brain cells.

Empire of illusion.
Literacy stagnant, scorned.
    Porn Queens strangled, despised:
        "whores," "cunts," "bitches."

Any hope? *Quien sabe?*
"Morning in America," three decades—
    a potent sedative.
    "Let them eat ketchup,"
        Saint Ronnie said.

Vietnam Christmas Recollected

what is this thing called love
that we hear about so tall
is it really from above,
not sublimated spite and gall

how can one believe his ears
can the rhyme be really true
for the sound of cash and carry
seems to bounce with I love you

at this season of good will
when the napalm takes a rest
how will the stock market respond
though Santa Papa does his best

so let the bells ring out with laughter
and the sound of peace on earth
in a little hour or after
men of stout heart will hymn the birth

and the righteousness that clothes us
like the spray that kills the leaves
will resume the extermination
of God's slant-eyed enemies

then the sound of joy will gladden
every throbbing righteous heart
and the market will recover
and the reign of love will start

let it come down like fall-out sparkle
settle impartially on mice and men
hail the love that guides the bullets
blesses cash and saves from sin

New World Order

for Ernesto Cardenal

"Hot damn, we're gonna
kick ass and get some pussy,"
my student told me—
that's what the young GIs say
as they're being sent to some land south of the border
where frijoles and rice build bodies
and Yankee efficiency is always in short supply,
as well as the Yankee dollar.

And I remembered
the words of an elderly Vietnamese
who spoke his peace in '68 or '69:
"You say you come to liberate us
but what you do,
you turn our children into pimps
our old people into beggars
our young men into revolutionaries
and our young women into whores."

And I thought of a character
in a play I've written,
whose rage smothers him like the breath
of a giant cockroach as he sweats in Reagan's
State Department, a mad Diogenes
with his army surplus Coleman lantern,
searching for an honest man.

"Ah, ha," my character reflected,
"there's a title for an article in *Foreign Affairs*—
"Kicking Ass and Getting Pussy:
American Foreign Policy in the Late 20th Century."

But kicking ass
is an old Yankee pastime,
not entirely unrelated
to the value of the Yankee dollar.
And you, Lt. Kilcourse,
writing in your journal
from near Ocotol, where the planes
of your comrades bombarded the town
ten years before the fascists leveled Guernica—
you, in your Marine uniform of 1927,
you knew the terms of this compact
between the gringo and the lesser breeds.
You did know, didn't you,
that North, South, East and West,
come what blood there may,
the gringo always, always,
always has to have his way.

So were you really so surprised
that the Nica president
sat in Managua "guzzling champagne"
surrounded by blond businessmen
while you and *your* men
fought jungle rot and lizards
for a chance to kick
Sandino's elusive ass?

When I found your journal
in the Marine Corps Archives
I also read a communique
in which they said
Sandino was a little crazy.
Naturally! Who but a madman
would object to the gringos
occupying his country
and turning it into
a plantation dependency,
with a first-class bordello, of course.

Whether you, Lieutenant,
among the other invaders
were "getting pussy"
I don't know,
but that's an old
military pastime, too—
even the Romans
must have gotten some.

Like ours, their empire was far-flung,
and I can hear now the "hot damn"
of a legionnaire from Ravenna
as he boards ship for Spain or Asia Minor
or the British Isles.

The Nazis didn't want to risk contamination
or share such obviously superior genes
with the "mongrel dogs" they conquered,
but we gringos, being more democratic,
have never been so fastidious.

When *glosnost*
showed its grinning visage,
promising peace and cooperation,
my character thought for sure
that at the Pentagon and the White House
they were burning the midnight Kuwaiti crude,
searching for a new enemy.
Imagine: almost an entire year
without a bona fide villain
to kick and, suddenly,
as if programmed by divine providence,
Saddam the Man, Hussein the Challenger,
dances onto the screen,
the All-American dream demon,
Allah's gift to General Electric
and McDonnell Douglas.

You, Lt. Kilcourse, missed the big show
but perhaps your grandson
writes letters over his desert coffee
or reads messages from home
(love-grams in the sand),
as he absorbs lessons in the old art
now perfected for the New World Order,
advertised, as "Ass Kicking Made Easy."

Those pilots, the media tell us,
have their own Super Bowl:
ass kicking at prime time,
pigskin and projectile
following the same clean trajectory,
toward goal post and factory chimney,
Yankee efficiency in laidback apotheosis.

Meanwhile, back in Paradise
the crowds descend on the gringos' Mecca,
where "Operation Desert Storm" T-shirts
and Old Glory perfume the Tampa air
and millions cling to flashes illuming the desert sky
(the Fourth of July in January),
as ass kicking by remote control,
murder by computer,
announce the birth of this,
the new New World Order.

Blood and oil mix,
the Dow Jones gyrates, then climbs,
the rape rate holds steady,
and I remember the look
on the face of a Czech student,
the hitchhiker on his way to Bratislava,
when he learned our nationality.
"Amerika *Über Alles"* was what he said,
only that: "America Over all the World."

And my character, who'd been picturing
the young students shouting "USA!" "USA!,"
and "We're Number One!" "We're Number One!"
hoped that at last they'd get it straight,
that message blowing in the wind
since it first echoed forth
from Montezuma's haunted halls:
"Amerika *Über Alles*!"

Epitaph for Ronald Reagan

How unlikely it seemed
that you'd sit where Washington,
Adams and Jefferson dreamed
dreams elastic and pristine.
They conjugated, like Latin verbs,
antique desires hot as sun
rays refracted through eyes that gleamed
when liberty and justice were won.
Their care was for us, and words,
the baggage of their train
of deeds, clasped hard upon
reality though again and again
interest sought to barter for quick gain
the truth they cherished much
and willed to us, wrought from pain.

You, a deformed shadow
of those you invoke,
use words like pigeons from a magician's hat.
You, the supreme lobotomist
for the millions who cannot bear to bear a thought,
the ultimate entertainer
schooled in every trick
of the alchemist's art.

You transform gold into pig iron,
declaring assassins the "moral equivalent of..."
him who year after famished year
faced the haughty Redcoats
with little more than valor and damp gunpowder?
Of him who forsook the beguiling Abigail
to pursue liberation from hated tyranny?
Of him whose words, like torches in the night,
guided the marchers through desert and swamp,
to Jordan's shielded shore,
noble Tom Jefferson?

From such roots came... what?
Came you?
Came you, assuredly,
the quintessential
modern American,
equipped with the requisite regalia
of imperial rule:
the obligatory, incurable ignorance.

Dixon's version of world history
that banishes the lesser breeds
to indistinguishable dustbins,
so that sixty years later
the blur is only partially
erased by seeing.

Came you, joining
the nonentities, criminals and dolts—
McKinleys, Nixons, and Coolidges,
Harding, the generous landlord,
Tyler, who couldn't do much damage.
But you, emperor of billions
with your script—
words, words, words;
grand illusionist,
all-purpose Houdini,
with your 16-millimeter reel of reality.
A passive purveyor
of others' desires
with only your genial innocence
to interpret our world:
what merchant of dreams
insatiable and rare
will redeem your swollen legacy?

By the wail of an overdue warning,
by suns that disperse blinding light?
And when the movie's done
 and the script's last word is read,
will addiction to your kind of fun
sustain only those already dead?

El Colonialisimo A La Mode

On the Costa del Sol,
where Spain reaches toward Africa
and the sun speaks many languages,
the English have a new colony
where you need speak
only one.

On every street and at every
corner (you won't hear *la esquina*)
pieces of England take root,
so that except for the sun
and the chambermaids who
won't look at you,
you might be at home:
London, Birmingham, Chipping Norton,
Bangor or Gloucestershire:
"Autos for Hire," "Houses to Let,"
"Live Entertainment."

In the Minimart at the Dona Lola Club,
three minutes from the beach
where the local fishermen
bring in *pez* and other
Mediterranean prizes,
a 10-ounce can of salmon
costs only 590 pesetas
less than 3 British pounds (£).

And "W," the made-to-order emperor,
needing no clothes.
    Subjects served by near-sighted optometrists.

Iowa voters, 2012 primaries,
"among the country's most sophisticated":
    media "wise men,"
        giving the time of day
    to a gang of buffoons, clowns, and frauds—
    America's intelligentsia.

And now, the long-awaited feature attraction,
    Barnum and Bailey's progeny,
        potty-trained by a drunken monkey.

Humpty Trumpty sat on a fence
his ample backsides covered by Pence.
    But the Russians grabbed him
        and shaved off his hair,
            lo and behold
                there was "no there there."

For such a tiny store,
it's surprisingly well-stocked:
tea biscuits (more than a dozen varieties),
corn beef, canned rice pudding, baked beans,
marmalade, and corn flakes—
even Spanish bread and an onion or two.

Javier, the driver of the jeep
that took us to a village
high in the Serrania de Ronda,
where a goatherd makes cheese
the way his ancestors did
when Ferdinand and Isabella hit the jackpot
with a cunning Italian sea captain,
thought it odd that the Brits seemed
incapable of expressing interest
in the life of the natives.

Imperialists everywhere, I said,
are much alike, all speaking a similar tongue:
"We count; you don't."

Land of the Free

In this land I loved
there is no censorship
and almost everything
is free.

The fragrance of daffodils
on cold April days
in Chicago
      is free.

And views of police
      strangling an unarmed
           black man in New York City
are free.

The squawks of crows searching
      for corn fields south
           of Calumet Harbor
are free.

The reports on TV of endless
      sectarian killings in Iraq
           for which we are not responsible
are free.

The laughter of Vietnamese children
      on the Ravenswood El
           just before it disgorges on Diversey
is free.

The reports of planned astronomical
          spending by several super-wealthy
                    citizens in the 2020 presidential race
are free.

The sunlight reflected
          off the breakfast-time
                    surface of Lake Michigan
is free.

The participation in the three-ring spectacle,
          which every four years reminds us
                    how free we are
is free.

The murmur of lovers
          on a hard bench
                    beside the Art Institute
is free.

The education that really educates
          about all the things free citizens
                    must know to be really free
is free.

The song about this land
          with its hammer and its bell
                    and its justice
is free.

The memories of clover fields
          turbulent with thudding bat
                    and smacking mitt
are free.

The board in a "correctional institution"
          for those who refuse to pay
                    for the training of assassins
is free.

The gleam in a child's eye
          after she has memorized
                    "The Little Red Hen"
is free.

The two square yards
          of cold concrete sidewalk
                    for those with nowhere else to sleep
are free.

The opportunity to have your brain
          scrubbed very clean
                    by the time you are eighteen
is free.

And the press, as they tell us,
          is exceedingly free
                    (though there were once
rumors of indescribably bloody horrors
          occurring in Guatemala, that the free
press decided, without consulting the free people,
not to reveal).

And four score and more years ago
our forefathers and foremothers
    brought forth on this continent
        a new nation
            where everyone is almost equal
              and they could
                not be more free.

III.

Intelectuales Apolíticos

by Otto René Castillo

Un día,
los intelectuales
apolíticos
de mi país
serán interrogados
por el hombre sencillo
de nuestro pueblo.

Se les preguntará
sobre lo que hicieron
cuando la patria se apagaba
lentamente,
como una hoguera dulce,
pequeña y sola.

No serán interrogados
sobre sus trajes,
ni sobre sus largas Siestas
después de la merienda,
tampoco sobre sus estériles
combates con la nada,
ni sobre su ontológica
manera De llegar a las monedas.
No se les interrogará
sobre la mitología griega,
ni sobre el asco

que sintieron de sí,
cuando alguien, en su fondo,
se dispone a morir cobardemente.

Nada se les preguntará
sobre sus justificaciones Absurdas,
crecidas a la sombra,
de una mentira rotunda.

Ese día vendrán
los hombres sencillos.
los que nunca cupieron
en los libros y versos
de los intelectuales apolíticos,
pero que llegaban todos los días
a dejarles la leche y el pan,

los huevos y las tortillas,
los que les cosían la ropa
los que les manejaban los carros,
les cuidaban sus perros y jardines,
y trabajaban para ellos,
     y preguntarán,
"¿Qué hicisteis cuando los pobres
Sufrían y se quemaba en ellos
Gravemente, la ternura y la vida?"

Intelectuales apolíticos
de mi dulce país,
no podréis responder nada.

Os devorará un buitre de silencio
las entrañas.
Os roerá el alma
vuestra propia miseria.
Y callaréis,
      avergonzados de vosotros.

Apolitical Intellectuals

by Otto René Castillo/ translated by Preston M. Browning, Jr.

One day
the apolitical intellectuals of my country
will be interrogated by the simple man of our people.

They will be asked
about what they did
when the nation
was slowly fading away
like a lovely blaze,
tiny and lonely.

They will not be asked
about their fine suits
nor about their leisurely
after-lunch siestas,
nor about their sterile
struggles with Nothingness,
nor about the ontological way
in which they
came by their wealth.
They will not be questioned
about Greek mythology,
nor about
their disgust with themselves
when one of their own,
out of his baseness,
chose to die like a coward.

They will be asked
nothing at all
about their absurd
justifications
nourished in the shadow of a fat lie.

That day
the simple men
will come,
those who never
fit into the books or the verses
of the apolitical intellectuals
but who spent all their days
bringing them milk and bread,
eggs and tortillas,
those who made their clothes,
chauffeured their cars,
took care of their dogs
and hoed their gardens,
always working for them,
and they will ask:
"What did you do
when the poor were suffering
and, consumed by pain,
all tenderness and life itself
were piteously burning away inside them?"

Apolitical intellectuals
of my dear country,
you will not be able
to utter a word.

A vulture of silence
will devour your guts.
Your own misery
will gnaw upon your soul.
And your shame
will seal your lips.

And when a spirited chronicle
of our time is written
by those who have not yet been born,
who announce themselves
with an expression
of fervent generosity,
we will exit that history
richer for having suffered it.
And surely one gains much
by enduring the pangs of his own time.

But it is beautiful
to love the world with the eyes
of those still unborn.
And how splendid
to already know oneself victorious
when all around one
is still so cold and so gloomy.

Viudo De Mundo

by Otto René Castillo

Compañeros míos,
yo cumplo mi papel
luchando
con lo mejor que tengo.
Qué lástima que tuviera
vida tan pequeña,
para tragedia tan grande
y para tanto trabajo.

No me apena dejaros.
Con vosotros queda mi esperanza.

Sabéis,
me hubiera gustado
llegar hasta el final
de todos estos ajetreos
con vosotros,
en medio de júbilo
tan alto. Lo imagino
y no quisiera marcharme.
Pero lo sé, oscuramente
me lo dice la sangre
con su tímida voz,
que muy pronto
quedaré viudo de mundo.

Widower of the World

by Otto René Castillo/ translated by Preston M. Browning, Jr.

My comrades,
I have performed my part
fighting
with the best that I have.
What a pity that the life
I had was so small
to face a tragedy so big
and to do so much work.

It does not grieve me
to leave you.
My hope remains with you.

You know,
it would have pleased me
to get to the end
of all this striving, with you,
to share in your wild rejoicing.
I imagine it
and do not want to go away.
But I know I must;
dimly my blood tells me,
with its timid voice,
that very soon I will be left
a widower of the world.

Palabras de Mujeres

by Francisco de Asís Fernández

Sólo quedan una que otra pared
simulando la casa
como escenografía de una obra de teatro
que representa el espectro de la muerte.

Por aquí pasaron los muchachos
todos rotos y remendados
gritando consignas
que hacían que se nos pararan los pelos de punta
y se nos brotaran las lágrimas.

Los ojos de los caídos
son como ventanas y puertas inmensas
abiertas para siempre.

Pasaron los muchachos
y nos llevaron a todos.
Y al ratito éramos nosotros
quienes levantábamos el vuelo de las palomas;
y almados y armados,
mientras disparábamos
entre órdenes y gritos de dolor
y consignas
que bien pueden valer lo que el más bello canto,
oíamos decir:

No hay mal que dure cien años
ni cuerpo que lo resista,
pero ya ven que el corazón aguanta menos.

Women's Words

by Francisco de Asís Fernández
translated by Preston M. Browning, Jr.
  and Susanna Ackerman

There are only one or two walls left
simulating a house
like the set of a play
representing the ghost of death.

Through here our boys came,
all scrapes and patches,
yelling out battle cries
which sent chills through our pores
and tears to our eyes.

The eyes of the fallen
are like windows and towering doors
open forever.

The muchachos came through
and they took us all with them
and a little while later
it was we
who were scaring the doves off,
armed and souled
while we were firing,
amidst orders, screams of pain,
and battle cries
  that might as well have been the most beautiful arias,

we kept hearing it said:
there is no evil which lasts a hundred years
nor a body that can bear it,
much less the heart.

Memoria del Sueño

by Francisco de Asís Fernández

a mis hijos Enrique Faustino y Camilo Reńe

Ahora que estoy vivo como la luz de una lámpara Coleman
(que imita la luz natural) y los veo dormidos como dos
   parajitas risueńos
entre las suaves depresiones de las almohadas
pienso que la vida surgió en la tierra solamente una vez
   hace 4000 millones de ańos
para que su madre y yo los engendráramos.
Sus sueńos, al igual que el mapa de mi mundo, no tiene
   menos amor ni menos dolor,
y 4000 millones de ańos fueron precisos para que
viviéramos esta escena de
      ternura.
Para estar aquí y ahora, hemos recorrido,
   ¿quien lo recuerda?
planicies, cráteres, cuencas, escarpadas, acantilados,
   arena volcánica,
roca fundida, rayos luminosos, desiertos rocosos,
   glaciares, *icebergs*, clorofilas,
      mares,
el descubrimiento de América y del Pacífico,
   la Australia y la Antártida,
el paso del Noroeste y del Noreste, el Polo Norte y
   el Polo Sur, el exilio y el hambre.

Nada detuvo a este hombre que somos, como
   una arenita en el Universo.
La tierra está a un segundo luz de la luna y
   a ocho segundos luz del sol
y el diámetro de nuestra galaxia para llegar
   a Alfa Centauris es de 90 mil años luz.
Esa arenita que somos, desde que desaparecieron
   los dinosaurios, hace 65 millones
         de años
ha recorrido el planeta como quien recorre el Universo.
Por eso velamos sus sueños.
Que nadie diga que todo sueño no es rico y
   perdurable por los siglos de los siglos:

Cuando mataron a Ricardo y a Camilo
Soñé que todos los días, mientras dormíamos,
mi mujer y yo nos transformábamos en tigres de Bengala
y con plumas de torcaz en las fauces, volábamos al espacio
a contemplar desde un punto del infinito,
   entre asteroides y meteoritos
las regiones iluminadas de la tierra.

Soñé que allí soñábamos, que entre rugidos y
   bostezos de aburrimiento
nos hartábamos los ojos, el corazón, las manos llenas
   de sangre y las vísceras del
         tirano.

Cuando ustedes despierten se darán cuenta que
   nuestro sueño se cumplió.

9 de febrero de 1983

Memory of the Dream

by Francisco de Asís Fernández
translated by Preston M. Browning, Jr.

to my sons Enrique Faustino and Camilo René

Now that I am alive like the light from a Coleman lantern
(which imitates natural light) and I see them sleeping
      like two smiling sparrows
between the soft depressions of the pillows
I think that life appeared on the earth only once
four billion years ago
so their mother and I could beget them.
Their dreams, just like the map of my world,
have no less love nor less sorrow,
and four billion years were necessary
so that we might live this moment of tenderness.

To be here and now, we have traveled through
      —does anyone remember it?—
prairies, craters, deep valleys, craggy mountains,
steep hillsides, volcanic sand, molten rock,
lightning flashes, rocky deserts, glaciers, icebergs,
      chlorophyll-seas.
The discovery of America and of the Pacific,
Australia and Antarctica,
the Northwest Passage and the Northeast Passage,
the North Pole and the South Pole, exile and hunger.

Nothing stopped this man that we are,
  like a grain of sand in the cosmos.
The earth is one light second from the moon
  and eight light seconds from the sun
and the diameter of our galaxy, to reach Alpha Centauri,
  is 90 thousand light years.
This tiny grain of sand that we are,
since the dinosaurs disappeared 65 million years ago,
has made its way around the planet
as we now go around the universe.
For this we watch over their dreams.
Let no one say that all dreams are not precious
and longlasting forever and ever.

When they killed Ricardo and Camilo
I dreamed that every day while sleeping
my wife and I were transformed into Bengal tigers
and with wild pigeon plumes on our jaws
we flew through space and from an infinite point,
amid asteroids and meteorites,
we contemplated the illuminated regions of the earth.

I dreamed that there we dreamed again,
that among groans and yawns of boredom
we stuffed ourselves full with the eyes, the heart,
        the bloody hands and the intestines of the dictator.

When you awaken you'll realize that our dream came true.

February 9, 1983

El Túnel

by Nicanor Parra/translated by Preston M. Browning, Jr.

Pasé una época de mi juventud en casa de unas tías
a raíz de la muerte de un señor íntimamente ligado a ellas
cuyo fantasma las molestaba sin piedad
haciéndoles imposible la vida.

En el principio yo me mantuve sordo a sus telegramas
a sus epístolas concebidas en un lenguaje de otra época
llenas de alusiones mitológicas
y de nombres propios desconocidos para mí
varios de ellos pertenecientes a sabios de la antigüedad
a filósofos medievales de menor cuantía
a simples vecinos de la localidad que ellas habitaban.

Abandonar de buenas a primeras la universidad
romper con los encantos de la vida galante
interrumpirlo todo
con el objeto de satisfacer los caprichos
 de tres ancianas histéricas
llenas de toda clase de problemas personales
resultaba, para una persona de mi carácter,
un porvenir poco halagador
una idea descabellada.

Cuatro años viví en El Túnel, sin embargo,
en comunidad con aquellas temibles damas
cuatro años de martirio constante
de la mañana a la noche.
Las horas de regocijo que pasé debajo de los árboles
tornáronse pronto en semanas de hastío
en meses de angustia que yo trataba de disimular al máximo
con el objeto de no despertar curiosidad en torno
  a mi persona,
tornáronse en años de ruina y de miseria.
¡En siglos de prisión vividos por mi alma
En el interior de una botella de mesa!

Mi concepción espiritualista del mundo
me situó ante los hechos en un plano de franca inferioridad:
Yo lo veía todo a través de un prisma
en el fondo del cual las imágenes de mis tías
  se entrelazaban como hilos vivientes
vormando una especie de malla impenetrable
que hería mi vista haciéndola cada vez más ineficaz.

Un joven de escasos recursos no se da cuenta de las cosas.
Él vive en una campana de vidrio que se llama Arte
Que se llama Lujuria, que se llama Ciencia
Tratando de establecer contacto con un mundo
  de relaciones
que sólo existen para él y para un pequeño grupo
  de amigos.

Bajo los efectos de una especie de vapor de agua
que se filtraba por el piso de la habitación
inundando la atmósfera hasta hacerlo todo invisible.
Yo pasaba las noches ante mi mesa de trabajo
absorbido en la práctica de la escritura automática.

Pero para qué profundizar en estas materias desagradables
qquellas matronas se burlaron miserablemente de mí
con sus falsas promesas, con sus extrañas fantasías
con sus dolores sabiamente simulados
lograron retenerme entre sus redes durante años
obligándome tácitamente a trabajar para ellas
en faenas de agricultura
en compraventa de animales
hasta que una noche, mirando por la cerradura
me impuse que una de ellas.
¡Mi tía paralítica!
Caminaba perfectamente sobre la punta de sus piernas
y volví a la realidad con un sentimiento de los demonios.

The Tunnel

by Nicanor Parra/ translated by Preston M. Browning, Jr.

I spent a period of my youth living with some aunts
due to the death of a man intimately linked with them
whose ghost disturbed them without mercy
making their lives impossible.

I paid no attention to their telegrams
or to their epistles written in the language of another era
full of mythological references
and the names of people I did not know,
several of them sages of the ancient past
and medieval philosophers of minor importance
and simple neighbors from their village.

To abandon all at once the university,
to break with the enchantments of a gallant's life,
to interrupt everything
in order to satisfy the whims of three hysterical old women
proved, for a person of my character,
a hardly gratifying prospect,
an idea utterly absurd.

Four years, nonetheless, I lived in The Tunnel,
sharing space with these fearsome ladies—
four years of constant martyrdom
from morning to night.

The hours of delight that I spent beneath the trees
were quickly turned into weeks of loathing,
months of anguish which I tried to obscure
as much as I could so as not to arouse their curiosity
  about me.
Those wasted hours became years of ruin and misery.
Centuries of imprisonment,
my soul languishing in the depths
of a bottle of wine.

My spiritualist conception of the world
put me in a situation of patent inferiority before reality:
I saw everything through a prism
at the bottom of which the images of my aunts
  were tangled like living threads
making a sort of impenetrable net,
which impaired my vision
causing it to be more and more ineffectual.

A destitute youth cannot interpret what happens to him.
He lives in a bell jar called Art,
called Lust, called Science,
trying to establish contact with a world of relationships
that exists only for him and a small group of friends.
Under the influence of a kind of water vapor

that seeped through the floor of my room
flooding the atmosphere until it made everything invisible.
I spent my nights at my work desk
absorbed in the practice of automatic writing.

But why go deeper into these disgusting things:
those matrons made my life a miserable joke
with their false promises, with their outrageous fantasies,
with their cunningly faked aches and
managed to hold me in their net for years,
tacitly forcing me to slave for them
on their farm
buying and selling animals,
until one night, peeking through a keyhole
I discovered that one of them,
my paralyzed aunt!
was walking perfectly, tiptoeing over the floor,
and with the emotions of a devil, I returned to reality.

La Víbora

by Nicanor Parra

Durante largos años estuve condenado a adorar
 a una mujer despreciable
sacrificarme por ella, sufrir humillaciones y burlas
 sin cuento,
trabajar día y noche para alimentarla y vestirla,
llevar a cabo algunos delitos, cometer algunas faltas,
a la luz de la luna realizar pequeños robos,
falsificaciones de documentos comprometedores,
so pena de caer en descrédito ante sus ojos fascinantes.
En horas de comprensión solíamos concurrir
 a los parques
y retratarnos juntos manejando una lancha a motor,
o nos íbamos a un café danzante
donde nos entregábamos a un baile desenfrenado
que se prolongaba hasta altas horas de la madrugada.

Largos años viví prisionero del encanto de aquella mujer
que solía presentarse a mi oficina
 completamente desnuda
ejecutando las contorsiones más difíciles de imaginar
con el propósito de incorporar mi pobre alma a su órbita
y, sobre todo, para extorsionarme hasta
 el último centavo.
Me prohibía estrictamente que me relacionase
 con mi familia.

Mis amigos eran separados de mí mediante
  libelos infamantes
que la víbora hacía publicar en un diario de su propiedad.
Apasionada hasta el delirio no me daba
  un instante de tregua,
exigiéndome perentoriamente que besara su boca
y que contestase sin dilación sus necias preguntas,
varias de ellas referentes a la eternidad y a la vida futura
temas que producían en mí un lamentable estado
  de animo,
zumbidos de oídos, entrecortadas náuseas,
  desvanecimientos prematuros
que ella sabía aprovechar con ese espíritu práctico
  que la caracterizaba
para vestirse rápidamente sin pérdida de tiempo
y abandonar mi departamento dejándome
  con un palmo de narices.

Esta situación se prolongó por más de cinco años.
Por temporadas vivíamos juntos en una pieza redonda
que pagábamos a medias en un barrio de lujo cerca
  del cementerio.
(Algunas noches hubimos de interrumpir nuestra luna
  de miel
para hacer frente a las ratas que se colaban
  por la ventana).
Llevaba la víbora un minucioso libro de cuentas
en el que anotaba hasta el más mínimo centavo
  que yo le pedía en préstamo;

no me permitía usar el cepillo de dientes que yo mismo
  le había regalado
y me acusaba de haber arruinado su juventud:
lanzando llamas por los ojos me emplazaba
  a comparecer ante el juez
y pagarle dentro de un plazo prudente parte de la deuda,
pues ella necesitaba ese dinero para continuar
  sus estudios.

Entonces hube de salir a la calle a vivir
  de la caridad pública,
dormir en los bancos de las plazas,
donde fui encontrado muchas veces moribundo
  por la policía
entre las primeras hojas del otoño.

Felizmente aquel estado de cosas no pasó más adelante,
porque cierta vez en que yo me encontraba
  en una plaza también
posando frente a una cámara fotográfica
unas deliciosas manos femeninas me vendaron
  de pronto la vista
mientras una voz amada para mí me preguntaba
  quién soy yo.
Tú eres mi amor, respondí con serenidad.
¡Ángel mío, dijo ella nerviosamente,
permite que me siente en tus rodillas una vez más!
Entonces pude percatarme de que ella se presentaba
ahora provista de un pequeño taparrabos.
Fue un encuentro memorable, aunque lleno
  de notas discordantes:

Me he comprado una parcela, no lejos del matadero,
  exclamó,
allí pienso construir una especie de pirámide.
En la que podamos pasar los últimos días de nuestra vida.
Ya he terminado mis estudios, me he recibido de abogado,
dispongo de buen capital;
fediquémonos a un negocio productivo, los dos,
  amor mío, agregó
lejos del mundo construyamos nuestro nido.

Basta de sandeces, repliqué, tus planes me inspiran
  desconfianza,
piensa que de un momento a otro mi verdadera mujer
puede dejarnos a todos en la miseria más espantosa.
Mis hijos han crecido ya, el tiempo ha transcurrido,
me siento profundamente agotado, déjame reposar
  un instante,
tráeme un poco de agua, mujer,
consígueme algo de comer en alguna parte,
estoy muerto de hambre,
no puedo trabajar más para ti,
todo ha terminado entre nosotros.

The Viper

by Nicanor Parra/ tranlated by Preston M. Browning, Jr.

For years I was condemned to adore a despicable woman,
sacrificing for her, enduring countless humiliations
  and jokes,
working day and night to feed and clothe her,
committing petty crimes,
robberies in the middle of the night,
falsifying compromising documents—
all for fear of being discredited in her fascinating eyes.
We would spend hours together in the parks,
hours of mutual understanding,
taking photos of ourselves while driving a motorboat
or we would go to a café
where we indulged in unrestrained dancing
lasting until the wee hours of the morning.

For countless years I lived as an enchanted prisoner
  of that woman
who would present herself at my office completely nude,
executing the most difficult contortions imaginable,
intending to incorporate my poor soul in her orbit
and, above all, extorting from me the very last cent.
She strictly prohibited me from having a relationship
  with my family.
She alienated my friends through infamous libels,
which this viper published in a newspaper she owned.

With a crazy passion she allowed me not one moment
   of peace,
peremptorily demanding that I kiss her
and answer immediately her stupid questions,
several concerning eternity and the future life,
subjects that created in me a distressing spiritual state—
a buzzing in my ears, frequent nausea and fainting spells.
With her very pragmatic nature she took advantage
   of my weaknesses,
dressing without losing a moment
and abandoning my apartment in such haste
   that I was left puzzled
and hopelessly disappointed.

This situation lasted more than five years.
For a time we lived together in a round room,
each of us paying half, in a luxurious neighborhood
   near the cemetery.
(Some nights our honeymoon was interrupted
as we were visited by rats entering through the window.)

This viper kept an account book
in which she recorded in minute detail
every last cent I had asked her to lend me.
She didn't even allow me to use the toothbrush
   I had given her
and she even accused me of having ruined her youth:
with her fiery eyes she urged me to appear before a judge
and pay within a reasonable amount of time
   part of my debt so that she could continue her studies.

As a consequence I was forced into the streets,
living on charity, sleeping on benches in the squares,
where the police would often find me almost dead
covered by the first autumn leaves.

Fortunately that state of affairs did not last long
because once I found myself in a square
while posing in front of a camera
when two delightful feminine hands suddenly
  covered my eyes
and a voice I loved asked, "Who am I?"
"You are my love," I responded serenely.
"My angel!" she said nervously.
"Permit me to sit on your lap one more time!"
Then I could see that she was dressed only
  in a small loincloth.
It was a memorable moment, though filled
  with discordant notes.

"I have bought a small piece of land,
  near the slaughterhouse," she exclaimed.
"I am thinking of building a kind of pyramid
where we can spend the last days of our lives.
I have finished my studies and am licensed as a lawyer,
I have a good amount of cash.
Let the two of us commit ourselves
  to a productive business, my love,
Building our nest far from the world."

"Enough of your rubbish," I replied,
 "I don't trust your plans.
Think for a moment of my real wife.
She could leave us in a state of abject misery.
My children are already grown up, time has gone by;
I feel profoundly exhausted, let me rest for a moment.
Bring me a little water, woman,
find me some food someplace,
I am dying of hunger.
I can't work for you anymore,
all has ended between us."

Recuerdos de Juventud

by Nicanor Parra

Lo cierto es que yo iba de un lado a otro,
a veces chocaba con los árboles,
chocaba con los mendigos,
me abría paso a través de un bosque de sillas y mesas,
con el alma en un hilo veía caer las grandes hojas.
Pero todo era inútil,
cada vez me hundía más y más en una especie de jalea;
la gente se reía de mis arrebatos,
Los individuos se agitaban en sus butacas
  como algas movidas por las olas
y las mujeres me dirigían miradas de odio
haciéndome subir, haciéndome bajar,
haciéndome llorar y reír en contra de mi voluntad.

De todo esto resultó un sentimiento de asco,
resultó una tempestad de frases incoherentes,
amenazas, insultos, juramentos que no venían al caso,
resultaron unos movimientos agotadores de caderas,
aquellos bailes fúnebres
que me dejaban sin respiración
y que me impedían levantar cabeza durante días,
durante noches.

Yo iba de un lado a otro, es verdad,
Mi alma flotaba en las calles
pidiendo socorro, pidiendo un poco de ternura;
con una hoja de papel y un lápiz yo entraba
  en los cementerios
dispuesto a no dejarme engañar.
Daba vueltas y vueltas en torno al mismo asunto,
observaba de cerca las cosas
o en un ataque de ira me arrancaba los cabellos.

De esa manera hice mi debut en las salas de clases,
como un herido a bala me arrastré por los ateneos,
crucé el umbral de las casas particulares,
con el filo de la lengua traté de comunicarme
  con los espectadores:
ellos leían el periódico
o desaparecían detrás de un taxi.

¡Adónde ir entonces!
A esas horas el comercio estaba cerrado;
yo pensaba en un trozo de cebolla visto durante la cena
y en el abismo que nos separa de los otros abismos.

Memories of My Youth

by Nicanor Parra/ tranlated by Preston M. Browning, Jr.

The truth is that I wandered aimlessly
  from one place to another,
at times bumping into trees,
colliding with beggars,
opening a path through a forest of chairs and tables,
with my soul on a thread
I saw the huge leaves falling.
But everything was useless.
I kept sinking more and more into a kind of jelly;
people laughing at my outbursts,
others turning restlessly in their seats to stare,
like seaweed moved by the waves,
and women casting in my direction hateful glances,
forcing me to exult, forcing me to despair,
forcing me to cry and laugh against my will.

All this led to a feeling of nausea,
led to a torrent of incoherent phrases,
threats, insults, uncalled-for swearing,
led to exhausting hip movements,
those funereal dances that left me breathless,
and made it impossible to get a steady footing for days—
and nights.

I wandered without purpose, that's certain,
my soul floating in the streets,
asking for help, asking for a little tenderness.
With a piece of paper and a pencil I went into cemeteries,
determined not to let myself be fooled by anyone.
I kept circling around the same subject,
I minutely observed everything
or in a fit of rage I tore at my hair.

In this state I entered classrooms,
like a wounded man I dragged along the floor,
crossed the threshold of private homes,
with a sharpened tongue
I tried to communicate with audiences:
some reading the newspaper
some disappearing behind a taxi.

Where to go then!
At that time the shops were closed.
I thought of a slice of onion I'd seen during supper
and of the abyss that separates us from all other abysses.

IV.

The Eyes of the Children of Solentiname
(The Island of San Fernando)

for Ana

The eyes of angels!
How else to describe the eyes
of these children, whose beauty
radiates like points of light
from a diamond, a ruby, a star?
These children as natural as Eve,
before that first delectable bite.

They dive into the lake like cormorants
searching for fish,
later stand at a workbench
wielding a machete—
to fashion a duck, a monkey, an iguana,
or absorb from a father, a sister, or a cousin
the skills of the artist,
creating paintings saturated with love
for the trees, the animals, the many-colored birds,
"primitive" art that assaults the viewer
with its simplicity and its authenticity.

Tucked into the southeastern corner
of Lake Nicaragua,
this island, which has a second name—
Elvis Chevarria, martyr of the revolution—
is the home of egrets, hibiscus, and lizards,
a place of peace and delight
where harmony is not a concept
in the books of theologians
or psychologists
but an experienced truth
alive in the eyes of *los niños*,
who may escape the miracles
of Disneyland and Hollywood
long enough to capture in paint
this other miracle—
the breathing, pulsating, singing
life of this demi-paradise.

Sound and Fury

nursery schools reverberate
young lovers celebrate
businessmen calculate
politicians just debate

beachcombers search the shore
stockbrokers lust for more
landlords screw the poor
pompous professors simply bore

prostitutes get up late
welfare patients sit and wait
lonely widows curse their fate
professional patriots merely hate

modulations of the heart
players wedded to a part

The Baptism

for Harvey Lord—in memoriam

One by one
they enter the pool,
in quest of new life
in heated primal waters.

Submerged, eyes not yet seeing,
like cave-bred bats,
tuned to sonar waves
that carry the sharp cries
of love or warning,
they embark upon this journey
through darkness
into . . .splash! . . .
Sunday morning light.

After this ancient rite,
what's washed away
and what's not quite?
What's too indigenous,
too Eveish and Adamish,
too like the marrow
in the original bone,
for supernatural medicines to atone?

When all is said and done,
the washing's one by one,
but the sinning,
as hot Augustine knew,
is frequently two by two.

The water settles,
lies quiescent,
while each newborn
reaches for a towel
and dry clothing—
sad fig leaves
to cover so much,
so much remaining.

3 AM

for C. M.

Luther said not works,
belief reveals His face;
we work until we drop,
insomnia is our grace.

Grandmother

for Cornelia Cabell Stephenson (1859-1926)
—in memoriam

You walked gently, I'm told,
those hard-scrabble acres,
your frame hardly fit
for the labor and grief it bore.

The farm, to which he brought
you young, a cunning thief
of your hopes,
and each fold
of your worn skirt
another reproach
to your sensitive soul.

And did you pine
for that other home
where the young gentlemen
from Mr. Jefferson's university
came for the holidays
to dance,
to woo,
to ask for
the hand of a sister
or two?

But you,
you had waited.

For what?
Only your stories,
romantic and melodramatic—
a young suitor slain just
as he approached his beloved's threshold—
in the best tradition
of the "ladies' magazines"
I think you devoured,
offer a clue.

Those and the one letter,
written to your sister
in middle age:
even the wedding night
an abrasive awakening—
a woman's lot,
to suffer
and always in silence.

Like Desdemona, you said,
and I thought
as I read your faded words:

you *knew*
before the first suitor,
elegant and correct,
had finished his
"Miss Cornelia . . . ."
you knew
from all you'd heard
and read
that he could not be It.

So you waited,
adding charms to your bracelet,
one for each terrifically
broken heart,
until all seventeen
together rang out the news
that the Right One
had arrived.

What made him right
I'll never know.
Perhaps his red hair
or was it a father's
opposition
that certified the choice?

I seem to hear
your voice
as you count the words
of "The Village Gossips"
or "A Blue Ridge Book Agent"
or as you warn the children
not to break the eggs—
those eggs you will hide
and later trade
for sugar and tea.

How you hated it,
the need
that drove you
to peddle cheap novels
and encyclopedias
to feed
his progeny
while he grumbled
and waited
for a king or an ace.

I contemplate your face
and speak your name,
vain efforts to know you.

If you could
come near, say,
by the large locust
beyond the spring house,
there's much I might ask,
though the answer
I most wish
you'd whisper in my ear
is to a question
you, I fear,
would find
most impertinent:
"Did he not,
in all those years,
if only once or twice,
lead you breathless
by the hand
to a place
where water tumbled
over mossy rocks
and dewy fawns
suckled a bright-eyed deer?"

Millennium Weather

I, too, have walked out in rain—
again, and again, and again.

That summer that was no summer,
when we waited sodden days
and bone-numbing nights
for the heat, so coy, so grudging
that by August we began to despair.

"Who knows," you said,
"maybe this is an appropriate beginning
for a new millennium,
one sure to be blighted
by weather fit for a stricken planet."

With no carpenter Noah in sight
we began to plan our escape.

"Go south, old man,"
you advised.
"Look for pecan trees and Spanish moss,
listen for 'Y'all' and 'Over yonder'
and sink new roots in the soil that nurtured you."

"Well," I replied,
"if the new millennium brings
only cloudy days and Julys that mimic January,
I'm stuck."

"Yankee stubbornness has invaded the bone
along with the cold
and the hills of Massachusetts
cry 'Home' to a heart that's been
restless for too long."

Managua '88

Her name was Zoraide
and I could never pronounce it correctly.
She was from Brazil
and I knew no Portuguese,
so we communicated in Spanish.

I called her simply
mi amiga chusca,
my droll friend,
and when she told me
that in South America
chusco means a vicious dog,
I was surprised,
for she was nothing like that.

Bottled Brotherhood: My Uncle Sam

for Charlie Browning

My Aunt Jenny "married down."
Was it a "shotgun wedding"?
I don't know but I'm pretty sure
my grandfather, Charles William Browning,
a successful upper middle-class farmer
and businessman, would never have allowed
his first-born and only daughter to marry
Sam Wood, from Woodville, Virginia,
a forgotten, one-mule burg—
not even a crossroads.

When Sam and Aunt Jenny were divorced
I don't know, nor when Sam came to live
in our town, Culpeper,
nor when he was overtaken by alcoholism.
My earliest and sole reliable memory
of this former family member is of Sam
sitting with the town's other winos
near the Southern Railway Station
in what was a sort of Negro section of town,
passing a bottle back and forth,
everyone, black and white, taking his turn—
Jim Crow be damned!

Had I the Poet's Ear

Had I the poet's ear, the sculptor's hand,
thy image fair in lasting form I'd cast,
and on this work I'd take my stand
content in thy reflection pure to bask.

For thine's a loveliness surpassing thought
that time alone may change or mar
and even time would find thee dearly bought
shining on forever, like a wayward star.

But I'm no Yeats nor Michaelangelo
only a poor rhymer whom some would scorn.
Nicanor Parra and his ilk might laugh "just so so,
you'll be a master when Gabriel blows his horn."

Yet still I'll sing thy praises till the last
and learn to blow a horn that's fit for lovers' joy
and bid you love and hold me fast
with passion true none can destroy.

Of all the joy and gladness
God sets before my view.
One, only one is flawless,
I think you know . . . it's you.

I Love To Spin a Rhyme

I love to spin a rhyme,
I'm not ashamed of it;
for steadiness and focus,
  it's like a horse's bit.

Milton surely did it
and another Brit named Donne;
I think there're many millions
who do it just for fun.

And so, old Señor Parra,
I tip my hat to thee,
your campaign against "pure poems"
called thousands to anti-chivalry.

But I'm an old man, too,
who cut his teeth on verse
that sings across the ages
to celebrate and to curse.

So I'll continue to read you
with reservations firm and true,
and hope you're in doubter's heaven
with a sign that reads "male shrew."

Elegy for an Eighty-Year-Old Southern Romantic

Like a troubadour
your soul sang of love,

love that ever flees,
as elusive as dreams.

Dreams beckon,
promising new life;
life quickens, pleading for new love.

Love is not the end, you discovered,
but the way, the way past
the bruises of childhood,
childhood that taught ambrosial lies,
like treacle, sweet and addictive.

When they took you to see Mae West,
those friends of your mother,
"Buxom Baker" and her fellow nurse,
you sat there in the semi-darkness,
your seven-year-old maleness
squirming in astonishment
at the miracle of breasts.

Ten years later you fumbled in the semi-darkness,
searching for what you never found.

There were breasts, all right,
but never what the breasts had promised.

Time caught you red-handed,
several lifetimes later, still amazed
at the sensuous beauty
your soul had sated itself upon.

"But love, love hides herself,"
waiting to be surprised
by him who knows her name.

Someone To Call You "Darling"

for Ann

Miracles don't grow on trees
nor in crevices of canyon walls.
You say "Darling" and I'm astonished,
after almost fifty years of hard knocks and anger,
tempered surely by tenderness and caring.
Yet "Darling"? "Darling," you say again,
and I say, but only in my heart,
"A miracle stopped by this morning and I,
well, I have learned enough
in seventy-seven years
to recognize its luminous garments."

With Gratitude

One of the great joys that comes along with publishing a volume of poetry, in addition to seeing the results of one's labors lodged between the covers of a book, is the opportunity for saying "Many thanks!" Offering thanks, if the gratitude is honest, can indeed be a source of immense pleasure. If one has lived a long life, especially in several different locales, the job can also be challenging. And if one has been the director of a retreat for writers, where well over a thousand individuals have spent days or weeks at a time working on a novel, a book of stories, a memoir, or a clutch of poems, the rigors of the task are magnified beyond calculation. Moreover, for those of us who have lived more than eight decades, the machinery of memory is generally in need of repair and often unreliable. Hence I undertake this exercise with a degree of timidity. On the other hand, since a number of those literary artists have through constructive criticism and/or enthusiastic support made positive contributions to the work at hand, and some have become valued friends, I experience the publication of *Sandino's Grave znd Other Poems* as a kind of collaborative celebration. Obviously I can here only thank a few of those who have contributed to its creation. Those I overlook will, I trust, forgive me. Of course, not everyone who deserves a word of thanks is—or was—associated with Wellspring House.

I begin with those who are no longer with us. Mac Moore was an adolescent acquaintance *only* who nevertheless got drunk with me some years later on the night before I went off, very reluctantly, to serve my country in the Army. It was September 1951, the height of the Korean War. I returned home four years later to find Mac with a wife, Harriet, and a baby girl with another on the way; Mac was also well situated in a D.C. suburban private high school teaching English. When I visited, we talked about mutual friends, family, and politics, but the conversation I slightly recall was one about contemporary fiction, books I had barely heard about such as *To Kill a Mockingbird*. So far as I can recall, this was my first exposure to literary dialogue but, since I was absolutely innocent of knowledge of the literary scene in New York or anywhere else in the country, there was precious little dialogue to be had.

I was impressed, however, by what I found in Mac and Harriet's company—a settled family with both members embarked on careers as teachers of language and literature, each with lively imaginations guiding their interactions with the world—Mac while teaching both painting and writing, Harriet teaching and writing while giving birth to and raising five children. I think it was the feelings evoked by observing friends living meaningful lives with the arts helping to add structure and purpose that made the lasting impression.

Mac eventually landed a position teaching both painting and literature at Woodberry Forest, a leading prep school in Virginia. With a pot of paint, a brush and an easel, he won the reputation of an outstanding teacher of painting. At a time when I, in my early twenties, was thrashing about with no idea of a career and little interest in literature, and surely no thoughts of a career as a teacher of literature—Mac challenged me and stimulated my interest in literary works far more challenging than the *Adventures of Mickey Spillane*, which I had devoured while in the Army. Mac Moore, now long dead, deserves in absentia a hearty embrace of gratitude.

Ben McKulec was one of the most eccentric humans I have ever known. Nor have I ever met a more passionate lover of poetry. When he was not reciting poetry—Chaucer or Milton or Keats or Whitman or Emily Dickinson—he was writing it. Or teaching it. His reputation as an English professor at York College in Pennsylvania was that of a brilliant master of the language who kept students on the edge of their seats waiting for his next burst of illumination as he unraveled one of Shakespeare's sonnets, for example. On a long and tedious two-day journey across France in a blizzard, Ben created for my daughters Katie and Sarah, then nine and seven, a miniature Greek/English dictionary. When Ben died in his fifties, I lost not only a friend but also an inspiring model—for teaching as well for writing.

I have fond memories and gratitude for the teachers: Ruth Lea Davies, Joe Mercer, Preston Roberts, and Nathan A. Scott, Jr., also in memoriam.

My deceased wife Ann was a consummate artist and I return periodically to her book *Deep Landscape Turning*—for wisdom, for mellifluous lines, and for a constant reminder of the joy that awaits those who truly love the English language and love making it ring after long labors. Ann cared deeply about the natural world and much of her poetry is devoted to celebrating its glories, all available to those who care to look. I think it fair to say that Ann taught me to see. By this I mean that, like many others in our society, I had virtually lost the capacity we all have as children to see things as they are, whether it be a tree, a house, or a bumblebee. As we grow into adolescence and then into adulthood, we more often than not "think about" rather than "see." Objects become lost in a swirl of abstractions, frequently to such a degree that we need a mentor to teach us to know the thing itself. And such knowing, if it penetrates deeply into the soul, is actually a kind of loving. Ann's poem, "Journey to Treskavic," illustrates that point to a T.

The scene is Macedonia where my family and I spent an academic year in the late seventies while I, with a Fulbright grant, taught American literature at the university in Skopje. On a Sunday afternoon we had come to visit a once-famous monastery and in the poem's first stanza Ann writes about how, struggling to catch up with the rest of the family that had gone ahead of her, she had slipped on gravel on the sheep path that led to the monastery and was startled to find inches from her nose an autumn crocus, a "petalled star rising from dust." In the second stanza, Ann performs a little poetic magic:

"Skirting its leaflessness/ I hurried along to catch the others./ What I know is that it came to be a part of me and rises now/ Balm, like honey."

Again and again in her poems, Ann takes the most ordinary kind of object from Nature or from human creation, and explores its "otherness," its capacity to reveal deep meanings within the human soul. Writing about such things as a wayside cross, a dilapidated church, a family house being emptied after its last resident has died, Ann invites her readers to share with her experiences both psychological and spiritual, experiences that may echo in one's consciousness for years.

During more than fifty years of marriage, Ann taught me countless things—about faithfulness, about forgiveness, about the utterly irreplaceable joys and values of family life. She also showed me in her practice the absolute necessity for the poet of certain virtues, principally among them, I think, patience.

Ann's and my daughter, Sarah, seems to have inherited from her mother that cardinal virtue but another as well—persistence. Every writer, to be at all successful, needs both. They also need courage. At age eleven, Sarah visited her grandmother, Marjorie Hutt, who was then living in Santa Barbara, California. Marjorie belonged to a poetry-writing group and Sarah, always willing to take risks, asked to join. Among these middle-aged and elderly women, according to her grandmother, Sarah was never fazed, writing and reading her own verses as if she were an established poet with at least two books to her name.

Sarah does now have two books to her name. The second one, *Killing Summer*, was produced while she was serving as Managing Director of Split This Rock: Poetry of Provocation and Witness. In this recent work, Sarah creates poetry out of three geographical contexts: Northfield Mount Herman School located in western Massachusetts, Petworth, a once-black neighborhood of Washington, D.C., and Rome, Italy. It is the second of these contexts that prompted the book's title, since a good deal of Sarah's poetry reflects upon the relentless murdering of black youth in cities such as Washington, D.C. Again and again, Sarah returns to slavery and other aspects of black history in America, almost as if haunted by the fact that her ancestors—my family—possessed humans in bondage.

Sarah has been exceedingly active in the D.C. area, organizing poetry-writing sessions for black youth, overseeing the many poetry happenings that Split This Rock offers to all comers in the city, and reading from her own works—and endless fundraising. In addition, she has been centrally involved in planning and carrying out the Ann Hutt Browning Poetry Series that takes place each spring in Ashfield, Massachusetts.

In addition, the bi-annual event that draws to Washington hundreds of poets and poetry lovers from across the country and indeed from Africa and Latin America as well, caps Sarah's achievements as a lover and producer of poetry, largely poetry that speaks for and from those who are the outcasts, the neglected, the exploited, and the forgotten in our society and other societies around the globe. Sarah's dedication to the quest for peace and social justice inspires me and helps sustain me in my own writing. I should also mention that some years ago she read and critiqued many of my longer poems. My dear Sarah, you make me a very grateful and proud father.

My older brother, Charlie, spent many years as a dairy farmer. Although he's quite intelligent and has had decades of psychoanalysis, he is in no way what you might call a devotee of great literature. Yet he is a key figure in my journey to a life devoted to teaching great literature. And struggling to produce poems and essays that others may enjoy.

In 1955, after years of debauchery at Washington & Lee, followed by several years of debauchery in San Francisco while stationed at the Army's Presidio, I returned home to Virginia like the "prodigal son" of Jesus' parable of that name, bankrupt financially, psychologically, and spiritually. Unlike the older brother in Jesus' story, Charlie welcomed me home and in fact rather took me under his wing. For almost one year, while I worked in our father's real estate office, Charlie, who was practicing the Christianity we had both been taught and which he had studied at the University of North Carolina after taking a degree in agriculture at V.P.I., fed me books: C.S. Lewis, W.H. Auden, T. S. Eliot, and other writers of the Anglican faith who yielded inspiring stimulation to my starved mind and soul. And I became hooked. I have never described myself as a "born-again Christian," but I did undergo a radical psychological transformation undergirded by a profound spiritual awakening. I began to find, in fact, in the plays, the poetry and the essays of these writers sustenance that led, in my case, to a new being. Soon I realized that I needed, and longed for, a serious education in the liberal arts. Where to study? The question was never one I spent time on. Charlie had extolled the University of North Carolina with such passion that, within several months of my decision to once again become a student, I was on my way to Chapel Hill to take a graduate degree in English literature.

One requirement of the masters in English was a thesis. At the instigation of Charlie, I had been reading for months the sermons and the poetry of an Anglican priest, Geoffrey Studdert-Kennedy, who wrote what might be called theology for the laity and poetry that was not likely to win prizes but acceptable as the subject of an academic study. For one summer I became preoccupied with research for a biographical chapter and one on the intellectual milieu out of which Studdert-Kennedy's poetry had emerged. Except for class papers, this was my first opportunity to write about poetry.

It's hard to imagine where I would have landed without the goading and the guidance of this affectionate and inspiring brother. Where I did land was surely in part Charlie's gift to his wayward sibling. "Charlie, boy," I thank you from the depths of my being. I admire and love you more than I can find words to express for what your respect and guidance have helped me to accomplish.

Like anyone else's life, a writer's life is marked by friendships, brief acquaintances, love affairs, chance conversations while riding on a train or bus, family stories and adventures, and a zillion other sources of "content." We may or may not carry with us a little book in which to jot notes but we carry in our heads a giant notebook filled with remembrances, especially of relationships with others. More important than the material that these relationships may oftentimes provide the writer for stories or poems are the emotional supports that everyone, perhaps especially the creative artist, needs. If we are lucky, we have memories of friends and acquaintances whose interest and encouragement kept us going through moments of near-despair leading to a feverish desire to chuck the manuscript and the Thesaurus into the nearest garbage can.

Though I've experienced many such moments, I didn't seek out a garbage can and so now I can undertake to thank a few of the dozens who have aided in the production of this book, some directly, most indirectly, by encouragement or challenge.

I begin with old friends: Bill Ryan and Jeanne Lightfoot, Nancy and Eben Tilly, Janet Gunn, Maynard Kaufman and Barbara Geisler, Leland Jamieson, Nancy Cirillo, and Giles Gunn. And move on to former students with whom I stay in touch: Matthew Baker, Juan Guerra, Boman Desai, and Rita Göndöcs.

Ashfield, Massachusetts, where I have lived for almost twenty years, is a charming village, chockfull of artists of many persuasions, with a poet on every corner as I say when describing the place where I live. Obviously an exaggeration, that phrase does capture the extraordinary artistic vitality of this "hill town" east of the Berkshires. Some examples: the Paris Press, founded and operated by Jan Freeman, is a feminist press devoted to bringing to today's readers female writers whose works may be largely forgotten; it's located on the outskirts of the town. The Double Edge Theatre, where reside and act some of our country's most brilliantly creative thespians, is a fifteen-minute walk from the center of the village. Actors Stacy Klein, Carlos Uriona, Matthew Glassman, and Jennifer Johnson are co-artistic directors of the ensemble. A dear friend, Kim Mancuso, who teaches drama at M.I.T., some years ago, directed a staged reading of a play I wrote while living in Chicago. We had an audience of more than seventy. Many thanks, Kim.

Our public library, where Martha Cohen creatively plans activities for all ages sponsors poetry readings twice a year.

Our monthly newspaper provides space for poetry in each issue. I am deeply grateful for *The Ashfield News*, whose editor, David Kulp, is a wonderfully creative person. Every year in the spring, the Ann Hutt Browning Poetry Series brings to St. John's Episcopal Church distinguished poets, who are introduced by the student who has taken highest honors in an area-wide competition. Six students read the poem they have submitted.

I might go on but I assume the point has been taken. If you live here and are a writer, you have company. As I intimated earlier, not everyone who falls on the list below has had a direct impact on my writing. But in a small community like Ashfield, a process of osmosis is inevitable. We influence and are influenced, often without knowing. So here goes:

Susan and Richard Todd; Lou and John Ratté; Mary Snow, Tom Snow, and Jill Riedan; Laura Rodley, Carlos Uriona, Stacy Klein, Stacy Adams, Jane Willis, Nan Parati, Addison and Jody Hall, Jody Stewart, Nancy and Laura of Ashfield Hardware, and Janet and Nort at Stead Lane Farm.

And also: Evan Barth, Marilyn Berthelettl, Margaret Bullitt-Jonas, Deanne Brochu, Ricki Carroll, Bob Carlton, Rosemarie Clark, Michael Corrigan, Susan Craft, Gordon Dean, Marc Fromm, John Hoffman, Herbert Libby, Mary Link, Nancy Marshall, Claire Mockler, Bill Nash, David and Virginia Newell, Phil Nolan, John and Cassandra Nawrocki, Donald and Molly Robinson, Mike Skalski, Beth Sperry, Hetty Startup, Kate Stevens, Abby Straus, William Spademan, and Jane and Jim Wagener.

To out of town friends too, a special thanks Rev. Vicki Ai, Peter and Libby Hutt, Lillian Jackman, Robert Jonas, Brenda Kennedy, Laura McGrew, Kathleen Miller, Mary and Bob Naftzger, June Nash, Bill Newman, Dori and David Ostermiller, Frank Reynolds, Pam Walker, Jennifer Walters, Richard Warner, Mark and Marie Zenick, and the members of the Standing Tree Affinity Group.

As noted earlier, of the former residents at Wellspring House, I can cite only a tiny sapling. I begin with Eileen Kennedy, who was one of our first residents and who has returned, I'm sure, more than fifty times.

Colleen Geraghty has for years been a regular at Wellspring House. In fact, her husband once came to check out the reason for her frequent absence from home, a sort of joke since he knew my age. Persons who know Colleen best describe her as "a force of nature" and someone whose compassion for suffering others is legendary throughout the county where she lives in Upstate New York. Colleen's support for my writing has been a blessing and she also brought to Wellspring House Sydna Burn who admires my work and has recently finished a fine book of haiku, many of which were written here.

Unexpected connections among writers attracted to Wellspring House spring up like dandelions in our front yard in May. My Virginia cousin Charlotte Davenport, after a couple of residencies here, introduced her poet friend Wendy DeGroat to Wellspring House, where she met Arlyn Miller. The two of them are soliciting poems about this residency or poems written here for a book to be presented on the occasion of the celebration of my 90th birthday in June 2019. I'm overwhelmed by such generosity of spirit everywhere I turn, something that helps an almost 89-year-old keep writing.

Others who for many years have come to write at Wellspring House who should be thanked are Tehila Lieberman, Jenny Barber, Jody Cothey, C. D. Collins, Mark Pawlak, Linda Cutting, Teresa Connelly, Susannah Cahalan, Denise Beaudet, Maya Liebermann, Shizuka Otake, Cathy Elcik, Aine Greaney, Erin Almond, Steve Almond, Jane Roper, Joe Fox, Geri Lipshultz, Bob Dahl, Theresa Bellone, and Fred McKinnan.

Now very close to home is Christian di Vitorrio who lived at Wellspring House for two years, helping with management but especially with my book, *Struggling for the Soul of Our Country*, as well as my poetry. A stunningly impressive poet, Christian was never reluctant to assist me in improving my own writing, whether poetry or prose.

Today I have the indispensible assistance of Jonathan Escoffery and Sarah Coldwil-Brown as writers-in residence and assistant managers at Wellspring House. In a variety of capacities, their assistance during the past year has been truly indispensible, and without their help neither Wellspring House nor I could continue to function effectively. Jonathan has read and reread my poetry, searching for errors, while suggesting improvements in diction, line length, etc., and has also devoted hours to searching through old folders for "lost" poems and translations. Working closely with Jonathan has been a creative experience that I will never forget. My debt to Jonathan is immense.

No less significant is my debt to Sarah, who has proved an expert in handling everything connected to promoting Wellspring House. She has oversight of many areas of our life together as the Wellspring House "family," for which I am deeply grateful. Thank you, Sarah.

A grand thank you for Judie Isabella for faithful service at Wellspring House.

When Catharine Clarke agreed to serve as editor of *Sandino's Grave and Other Poems*, I knew I was fortunate. I did not know, however, just how fortunate. With years of experience and a consummate understanding of the full range of complexities involved in editing even a small volume of poetry, Catharine has been the kind of editor any writer might wait years to engage. She has promised me a beautiful book and a beautiful book she has produced. Her patience with my delays and her sensitivity to my indecisions and hesitations have been remarkable. My gratitude, Catharine, for your enthusiasm and your skill knows no bounds.

Finding the words to adequately thank a family such as mine is difficult. Katie, Sarah, Rachel, and Preston III, for your generosity of heart, your faithful support, your never-wavering affection, and your deeply rooted ability to inspire me with your talents and dedication to applying them for the common good—for all these I feel truly blessed and offer profound gratitude. And to the progeny—Ben, "Miss Gracie," Sam and Dakota—such extraordinary grandchildren, to each of you I offer a thousand thanks for your talents, your enthusiasm for life, your kindness, your steady love, and your faithful commitment to the happiness of the Browning family.

And, finally, to my dear friend Janet Brof for her loving support.

About the Author

Preston M. Browning, Jr., a retired English professor, has published three books: *Flannery O'Connor: The Coincidence of the Holy and the Demonic in O'Connor's Fiction*, *Affection and Estrangement: A Southern Family Memoir*, and the most recent, a collection of ten essays entitled *Struggling for the Soul of Our Country*. He has been writing poetry for decades, with poems appearing in The Friends Journal, Phase & Cycle, The Pikestaff Forum, The Ecozoic Reader, and other journals. In the late seventies Browning and his family spent an academic year in Macedonia on a Fulbright grant to teach American literature at the university in Skopje. He is the owner and director of Wellspring House: A Retreat for Writers and Artists in Ashfield, Massachusetts.

Ordering and Contact Information

To place an order directly from Wellspring Press, email: info@wellspringhouse.com

Sandino's Grave and Other Poems is also available online via Amazon, Barnes and Noble, and other online retailers.

To reach the author, you may email him at browning@wellspringhouse.net or write him at Wellspring House, P. O. Box 2006, Ashfield, MA 01330.